Jubilee 2020

Carmine Gorga

CIP a Camerei Naţionale a Cărţii

Gorga, Carmine

Jubilee 2020/Carmine Gorga. – Chişinău : Generis Publishing, 2020 (Print on demand).– 87 p.: fig.

Referinţe bibliogr.: p. 75-79.

ISBN: 978-9975-3421-5-5

330.1

G 70

Cover Image: www.pixabay.com

Online orders: www.generis-publishing.com
Orders by email: info@generis-publishing.com

Books by the Author

The Redemption of the Bully: Through Love, Toward the Beloved Community.
Scholars' Press, 2018.

The Economic Process: An Instantaneous Non-Newtonian Picture Third Edition,
The Somist Institute, 2016.

The Centrality of the Resurrection: Are We Ready to Let Jesus Enter our Hearts?
(Relationalism) (Volume 2), The Somist Institute, 2016.

A Case for God: In Search of a Humanism Filled with True Human Beings,
(Relationalism) (Volume 1), The Somist Institute, 2014.

The Economic Process: An Instantaneous Non-Newtonian Picture. Lanham, Md. and
Oxford: University Press of America, 2009, expanded softcover edition.

To My Polis, With Love: May Gloucester Show the World the Ways of Frugality, The
Somist Institute, 2008.

To My Polis, With Love: May Gloucester Show the World the Ways of Frugality, The
Somist Institute, 2008, Kindle edition.

The Economic Process: An Instantaneous Non-Newtonian Picture. Lanham, Md. and
Oxford: University Press of America, 2002.

Quality Assurance of Seafood (with Louis J. Ronsivalli), Van Nostrand Reinhold,
1988, hardcover.

The paper was tight and consistent. It deals mostly with the "ought" rather than the "is" as I view human nature and history. I've no objections to the values and internal logic.

Steve Kurtz, an investment banker

You have written a truly monumental paper... Only one very, very small minor point separates us. I feel your criticism of Adam Smith is too harsh....

Prof. Michael E. Brady

I finally got a chance to read your text and it is indeed an incredibly original treatment of the whole issue. I have to read it again to understand some of the economic points, but the overall historical and moral treatment was immediately within the layman's reach and very impressive. Congratulations!

Prof. John C. Rao

Thank you for your stimulating paper. It is evidently full of stimulating and valuable ideas. Since I have not done any work on these matters, there is nothing I can add aside from my best wishes.

Prof. William J. Baumol

Have you taught? I think you have; you teach the reader, or make the reader pause and reflect on how beautifully simple life could be.

Teresa Arnold, a social worker

Your objectives are worthy and I also share.

Rabbi Myron S. Geller

Dedication

No work stands alone. The reader will gradually discover that this work is uniquely due to actions and thoughts of many, most notably Moses, Jesus, Aristotle, Thomas Aquinas, the Doctors of Salamanca, John Maynard Keynes, Benjamin Franklin, Henry George, Luis D. Brandeis, and Luis O. Kelso.

My hope is that I have faithfully listened and transcribed.

My peace of mind rests on the open availability of the texts I have perused.

Table of Contents

Acknowledgments

Special thanks for the original publication of these works go to

- ✓ *Econintersect,*
- ✓ *Nova Science Publishers, and*
- ✓ *ssrn.*

<h1 align="center">A Plea</h1>

In the name of Moses and of sanity, CANCEL ALL DEBTS. Declare a Debt Jubilee, Jubilee 2020. Apart from strengthening the social welfare net, there are other measures to consider in order to assure long-term recovery. But they can wait.

In the extraordinary events of these days, we must take extraordinary measures. To the list of important proposals under consideration, the Congress of the United States and Governments the world over might heed this plea: Please, cancel all debts.

This measure will *keep* cash in the pocket of consumers, cash *ready to spend.* Hence, it will keep many businesses open; many jobs now performed well will be preserved.

This measure will add tranquility to many stressed minds.

This is a measure whose wisdom is justified not only by the arguments examined in the following pages concerning Moses' Jubilee. This is a measure whose wisdom is justified by long-standing, deep research by Professor Michael Hudson. In his new book, *...and Forgive Them Their Debts,* Professor Hudson points out that the proclamation of debt jubilee—on all but some business loans—has indeed been a reality, not only in ancient times and especially in ancient Israel; universal debt jubilee has been practiced at the installation of every Emperor or King whose heart was in the welfare of the entire nation. And the entire nation loved that sovereign accordingly.

Just consider this slide:

Is it not true that, *if their relative relationship is constant,* **it does not matter one iota** whether two people or two social classes have hundreds of dollars, millions of dollars, or trillions of dollars in their accounts? Wealth is a *relative* social entity. Keep the relationship stable, and if you cancel debt systematically you destroy only a number of **zeros**. *Real wealth* of bread, tables and chair as well as human relationships remain totally undisturbed. They remain safe and sound. Indeed, they remain more safe and more sound than before because, once freed of the burden of debt, the debtor is free to create more wealth for himself and others.

There is another way to look at the wisdom of Moses' Jubilee. Let us just consider the true meaning of money.

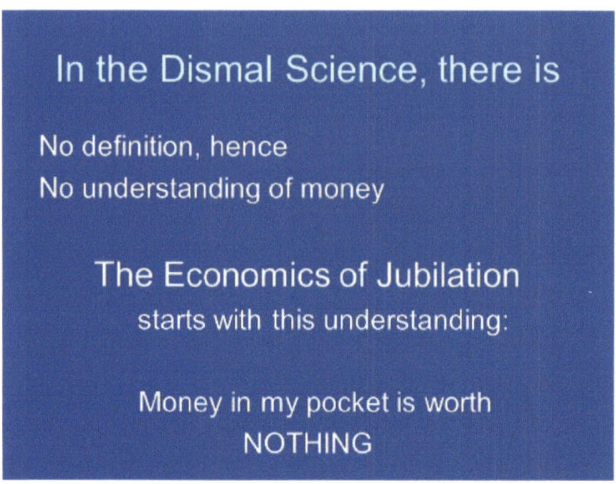

Money acquires its value in the exchange:

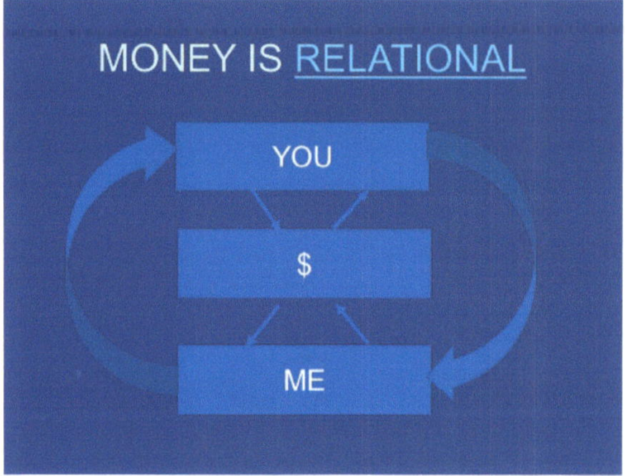

Money has only an exchange value. Money shows its true value when the debtor is alive. So, in extraordinary times let us use extraordinary measures that will set millennia of misunderstandings aright. Let us use our current crisis as a great opportunity to cancel all debts systematically at once—and observe the wisdom, the Mosaic wisdom, of cancelling debts cyclically, during the course of every seven years.

Good ideas are not implemented because they are good; they ae implemented because good people push for their implementation. Do talk with your state and federal representatives about the need for an immediate cancellation of debt. To keep us united, and aware of our progress in the meantime, please study and sign this Internet petition:

DEFUSE THE BOMB http://petitions.moveon.org/sign/the-jubilee-solution, the bomb of a financial crash at any stage in its development.

Chapter 1: The Lender Is Not A Hoarder.
And What Is Interest?

I am not a Jew.

How to staunch the river(S) of opprobrium poured over the head of the lender during the last 5,000 years of recorded history?

The Lender Is Not a Hoarder

Even Shakespeare got into the act. Who can forget Shylock? To understand Shakespeare, we have to put him within two bookends: The near universal misquotation of the First Epistle of Paul to Timothy and the forgery of the Protocols of the Elders of Zion. The details are too well known and too painful to recite here.

The first obvious observation to make, and to stress, is that not all the lenders are Jews.

Period.

The second observation to stress is that neither Shakespeare nor those who misquote Paul are economists. They <u>simply do not know what they are talking about</u>. They know not <u>what money is</u>.

A silly point. I am not a Jew. I am not writing this long overdue re-evaluation of the lender because I am a Jew and somehow want desperately to put the record of antisemitism straight at least as the lending of money is concerned.

No. My evaluation of the lender is based on the study of <u>Concordian economics</u>. Through Concordian economics it becomes exceedingly clear that the lender is not a hoarder.

The long bill of particulars <u>against the hoarder</u> is not of concern here.

The long bill of particulars in favor of the lender can be shortened here by asking: Would the world be better off if people with money, people with money who do not have an immediate use for it, were to hoard the money? The question answers itself.

What Can We Demand of the Lender?

No, I am not going to proffer an indiscriminate approval of the actions of the lender. Especially after witnessing the abuses of the lending power of large corporations committed before the last financial crash, when loans were approved for people who could clearly not sustain the load, but nonetheless offered a variety of immediate profits to the lender, it is evident that "society" must demand that the lender use judgment in the evaluation of the loan.

The lender has responsibilities.

Loans that have minimal chance of being repaid ought not to be issued at all. I wonder whether society will ever find adequate sanctions against irresponsible lending practices, but we can certainly summarily spotlight them and condemn them at will

The second condition through which society must evaluate lending practices is the amount and form of interest to be applied to a loan. To answer these questions appropriately, we need to know what interest is.

What Is Interest?

Interest, Keynes said, is "the reward of not-hoarding." Keynes, of course, is the supreme economist of the last century. The dead economist who controls our lives. All mainstream economics is based on his fundamental book titled the General Theory; all heterodox economics, in its various shapes and forms of "post-Keynesian" economics, as well as Austrian economics, is all economics written "against Keynes."

In the meantime, no one has paid attention to Keynes' definition of interest, because <u>no modern economist understands what hoarding is.</u>

Rather than demanding an effort to understand hoarding, I will be satisfied if the reader makes an effort to understand interest. Benjamin Franklin knew, he understood what interest is, and welcomed it. Did he not famously say something like:

"I'm glad to give the other fellow 5%, if I can earn 6%."

But notice that our Beloved Benjamin, if my love for him gives me permission to be so disrespectful, was talking of capital credit - not the abyss of consumer credit into which we have lately plunged. Consumer credit is only fruitful for the lender. Yet, the loan agreement is entered voluntarily; apart from advocating for education about economic affairs, there is nothing that economics can do to save the borrower and make the consumer loan productive ... unless one approaches the situation indirectly ... unless the <u>"cash-back" movement</u> becomes truly widespread, unless capitalism becomes truly responsive to the needs of consumers - and its own survival - and so responsible as to elect representative consumers to the Board of Directors of modern business corporations through the legal institution of Consumer Stock Ownership Plans (CSOPs).

That is it. With capital credit, interest is the fruit of the use of other peoples' money. With consumer credit, interest is giving to the lender the fruit of one's own future productivity: A totally destructive activity; how many enterprises are undertaken, how many trees are felled to pay interest on consumer credit? The principal in consumer credit is never likely to be paid back.

And yet, does not the consumer derive the benefit of immediate use of real goods and services? Don't we live in the moment? It might be vain to ask: What's the rush?

To summarize, apart from the abyss of consumer credit, with a loan agreement voluntarily entered into by the majority of the population, would society be better off if money remained in the pocket of a person who does not know, or does not want to go through the pain of making money bear fruit?

Let the lender be finally praised.

Two Caveats

This is not an idiosyncratic blessing of interest. There are two important caveats that I should attach to the unjustly vituperated 5,000-years-old practice of lending money at interest. The first caveat is that society should forever be on the alert against exorbitant interest. My brain is too small to define what an exorbitant rate of interest is. But my heart knows it when it sees it. Yes, my heart bleeds a bit at that sight.

Where blood gushes out of my heart is at the mention of compound interest. I cannot find any justification for compound interest, except in the power of the lender and the power of mathematics. To elaborate on the power of the lender, especially the political power of the lender is fruitless. It will forever be exercised, whether openly or through the subterfuge of clever lawyers and accountants - and legislators, should I whisper?

What must be open to discussion is the justification for compound interest. I find none. Let us run a small thought experiment, an experiment whose conclusions can be easily tested through the inordinate intellectual and financial power of the modern University. Let us pose this alternative to a "perfect" representative sample of lenders: What is fairer, Simple Interest - with its linear growth pattern - or Compound Interest, with its exponential growth pattern?

My suspicion is that most people, to repeat, most lenders, will agree that the linear growth rate is fairer than the exponential growth rate.

Will this exercise become the seed to set loan agreements on a just and sustainable basis? Let us shortly find time to give some undivided attention to the issue. Let us not sheepishly accept diktats from the past.

If this solution is not chosen, especially because its implementation is surely going to be a slow process, rather than advocating a vainglorious attempt to curb the power of individual lenders, let us see what can be done, systematically - as a society.

A Fruitful Curb of the Power of the Lender

Yes, the modern world - ah, Progress, Enlightenment, Reason, and all that - is bereft of defenses against the power of the lender. We have no intellectually solid, no morally valid defense against the power of the lender.

It is scouring the past that I have unearthed "the" solution: The Jubilee Solution. The Jubilee Solution is a systematic cancellation of all debts on the eve of the Jubilee Year. The Jubilee Year starts at the end of the seventh year.

There are various forms of jubilee. There is the Seven Day Jubilee regarding Time; the Seven Year Jubilee regarding the tillage of the Land; and the end of the 7x7 = 49 Year Jubilee regarding Stewardship of the Land. These are all extremely important manifestations of Jubilee, jubilation of the heart. This encompassing vision is too much for one lazy morning. Let us concentrate our attention on the Seven Year Jubilee regarding debt.

Much to say. Compressed, it is this: It is only money, people; it is only money that, remaining in the pocket of the lender, would most likely be hoarded; it is only money that is keeping the debtor in knots; it is only a set of zeroes that, once cancelled from the accounting books, make everyone free to start a new life as a productive agent again. (Have not modern venture capitalists learned not to shy away from first, and second, and even third failure? If the borrower has used the painful experience to learn how to succeed, why waste all that learning?)

It was Moses who legislated the Debt Jubilee. It was Jewish society that had the intellectual talent to see the wisdom of the Debt Jubilee and the moral stamina to practice it every seven years. Cynics doubt the debt Jubilee was ever practiced. I personally do not care whether it was practiced even once and Michael Hudson has provided an unobjectionable wealth of evidence of the soundness of this solution in the number and quality of copycats: Every Emperor, every King - well, most Emperors, most Kings; many Emperors, many Kings ? - upon installation has declared a Debt Jubilee.

Moses was a Jew. And Jesus did not ever contradict Moses, but he asserted his readiness to fulfill the mission of Moses and the Prophets. In the words of Paul, Jesus did not say that money is the root of all evil. The correct quotation is

"Love of money is the root of all evil."

Love of money is the root of hoarding and, in the Parable of the Talents, Jesus, uncharacteristically, sends the hoarder straight to Hell: No trial; no appeal.

Yes, I am not a Jew, but I am very proud to acknowledge my intellectual debt to Moses, and to Jesus.

Chapter 2: THE ECONOMICS OF JUBILATION
Blinking Adam's Fallacy Away

Abstract

A system of thought allowed for the free market price of land to cyclically go down to zero. This is the economics of Moses. The economics of Jesus is a restatement of the economics of Moses. The first was applied during Biblical times and the latter, united with Aristotle's thought and transformed by the Doctors of the Church into the doctrine of economic justice, was applied over vast territories up until the late Renaissance. With the assistance of Concordian economics, the mathematization of the Parable of the Talents leads to an opportunity to adapt those two ancient economic perspectives to the complexity of the modern world. In so doing one blinks Adam's Fallacy and the subsequent mainstream economics away.

Acknowledgments

The framework of analysis on which this paper draws is uniquely due to 27 years of exhaustive probing by Franco Modigliani and 21 years of assistance from Meyer L. Burstein. Mitchell S. Lurio and Norman G. Kurland have been great teachers of economic policy. Technical assistance was offered by Charles F. Schibener, III. Much encouragement was continuously provided by Alan Reynolds, Raymond G. Torto, and John K. Skank. Otto Eckstein, Frank L. Cooper, Steve H. Hanke, and Harry G. Johnson were the first economists to confirm that the revised Keynes' model was consistent. I also would like to acknowledge a clarification brought to this paper by Godfrey Dunkley. Helpful comments, suggestions, and recommendations on earlier drafts of this paper were tendered by a number of referees as well as by William J. Baumol, Michele Boldrin, Jeroen C.J.M. van den Bergh, Kevin P. Gallagher, William J. Toth, William R. Collier, Jr., Michael Emmett Brady, and Myron S. Geller. Selective portions of this analysis have also been endorsed by John K. Galbraith, Mark Perlman, Francesco Forte, Augusto Graziani, Alberto Tarchiani, Aldo Garosci, Giorgio Spini, Gerald Alonzo Smith, Charles T. Wood, Norman A. Bailey, Buckminster Fuller, Rosanna Marini, Gordon

Richards, Rudy Oswald, Steve Kurtz, Ernest Kahn, Louis J. Ronsivalli, Howard Zinn, Robert F. Drinan, Thomas J. Marti, Cassian J. Yuhaus, James E. Hug, Richard John Neuhaus, John J. Neuhauser, Irving Kristol, Michael J. Naughton, and John C. Rao among others. Thanks for editorial assistance go to Jonathan F. Gorga and David S. Wise.

Analysis reveals the existence of a body of doctrines that can be properly classified as the economics of Moses and the economics of Jesus: a delicate balance of economic rights and economic responsibilities. Astounding as this proposition sounds at first hearing, these perspectives shed a unique light on about three thousand years of economic literature and practice. To appreciate the inner coherence of this body of doctrines, it is necessary to treat them separately. Part I of this paper attempts to reconstruct the economics of Moses; Part II the economics of Jesus. Part III presents conditions through which these doctrines can be interjected into the complexities of the modern world.

The economics of Moses is contained in two fundamental doctrines: *Observe Jubilee* (including Sabbath and Sabbatical year) and *Do Not Steal*. The first is enunciated in Ex 20:8-11; 34:21; Lev 23:3; 25:2-16, 23-28; Num 33:53-54; 34; and Deut 5:12-15; 15:1; the second in Ex 20:15 and Deut 5:19. We shall see that these two doctrines embrace the whole of economics.

The economics of Jesus is a restatement of the economics of Moses and is contained in three fundamental doctrines. Two complementary doctrines are derived from the Parable of the Talents in Mt 25:14-30: The first doctrine states, *Invest Your Talents*; the second states, *Do Not Hoard*. The third is enunciated in Mt 22:21: *Give to Caesar What Is Caesar's*. We shall see that these three doctrines contain the whole of economics.

Both sets of doctrines contain the whole world of economics, because—rather than starting from the economics of the household, as the Greeks did—they both address the whole of the economic process, which, as established by Classical economists, contains, not the market exchange of two commodities, but the study of the production, distribution, and consumption of wealth of an entire nation or the world as a whole. Of course, both Moses and Jesus explain theory and policy in accordance with the exigencies of the historic moment of their time. Hence, what changes is not the substance of the discourse but the response to immediate needs and the literary expression. As we shall see, the content of the doctrine of the Jubilee is the same as the content of the doctrine of Not Hoarding; and the content of the doctrine of Not Stealing is the same as the content of the doctrine of Giving to Caesar what is Caesar's. In Moses the injunction to invest is implicit; in Jesus this injunction is explicit.

The reason for the last difference becomes clear when it is placed in the context of modern economic theory. From Adam Smith (if not from Locke or even the late scholastics) onward, it has become axiomatic that freedom is a condition of economic growth. Give people economic freedom, and moral, normal people will invest their talents in the most productive way that is open to them. The operation of the butcher and the baker, the creation of a symphony, just as the creation of a useful gadget or a financial derivative, are included in the use to which God-given freedom (see esp. Gen 3:22; Ex 8:1-32; and Gal 5:13) can be put in our world. From which one must deduce, and history confirms, that by the time of Jesus people had lost most of their natural economic freedom. Hence Jesus had to make explicit the need to invest one's talents.

Naturally, both Moses and Jesus are deeply concerned with the condition of the poor, the marginalized, those who—for any reason—are excluded from the blessings and burdens of participating in the economic process. We shall see that giving to the poor is an implicit aspect of the Jubilee and an explicit aspect of the doctrine of not hoarding. Yet, giving to the poor is not an economic doctrine; it is a moral injunction. Transfers of wealth from the rich to the poor, just as transfers from the poor to the rich, do not form an economic doctrine. They are moral—or immoral—practices: They are moral, if voluntary; they are immoral, if involuntary and forced. Unrecorded, there is much voluntary giving from poor to poor and from the poor to the rich, which the rich are always willing to accept. Such is the way among human beings.

Part I — The Economics of Moses

The two economic doctrines of Moses are: *Observe Jubilee*; *Do Not Steal*.

1. Observe Jubilee

What is the doctrine of the Jubilee? There are many facets to this doctrine which lie outside the scope of this paper (cf. Harris 1996; Trocmé 1973). Our focus is on its economic content. This is an economic doctrine and practice of subtle complexity. There are three aspects to it: one concerns land; the other concerns money; the third concerns products-things-time.

Jubilee Concerning Land

Economists might want to study the medium term injunction of the Jubilee, liberally extended to cover the Sabbatical and everyday practices. This is the injunction to leave the land fallow every seven years—to let it organically rest so that it will recover its powers naturally, rather than force feeding it with chemicals. (Because of the savings involved in any reduction of chemicals and smaller external costs of clearing the effects of chemicals from the waters downstream and eventually the water table, economists may wish to give this practice more than a fleeting glance. The appetite for the economics of pesticides might be wetted by the knowledge that pesticides—while harming human health and the ozone layer—are used, not to enhance the productivity of the land, as to eliminate blemishes from the produce appearance.) Here we are concerned with the long term economic—and, necessarily, legal and moral—aspects of the Jubilee in relation to the land. By the end of the 49th year, the doctrine calls for the return of the land to the original possessor. Hence, on the 50th year—the Jubilee year—the slate is clean. Just as with the U.S. Homestead Act of 1862 or in the Amish community and Bali today, the original possessor acquires land at no cost (Num 33:53-54; 34), a gift from inheritance. The responsibility is to till the land. The purely economic aspects of the Jubilee are revealed by the practice of purchase and sale of land during the forty-nine years preceding the Jubilee; by the existence of price; and by the existence of market. These three aspects are coordinated to such an extent that, with passage of time, the price of the land—astonishingly—goes progressively *down* to zero the closer one gets to the year of the Jubilee (see Lev 25:13-16; 27:16-24). These three aspects bear deep examination. And they can be better understood by indirection. Purchase and sale of land could have been prohibited; and there would have been no market, and thus no price. The price mechanism of the Jubilee calls for close attention. Since the price of land decreases with the passage of time, the arrangement reveals that there was the observation of an inner coordination of events in the application of the Jubilee: first, everyone obeyed the mechanism; since there is no evidence of compulsion, everyone obeyed it voluntarily; and since the price of the land decreased over time, it was clearly responding to a framework of economic analysis. What was this framework? The process of price determination becomes reproducible and decipherable as one looks at the economic, the legal, and the moral context into which the purchase and sale of land was taking place.

The Economic Context. To see the various relationships involved in the institution of the Jubilee, it is useful to build the following analytic framework:

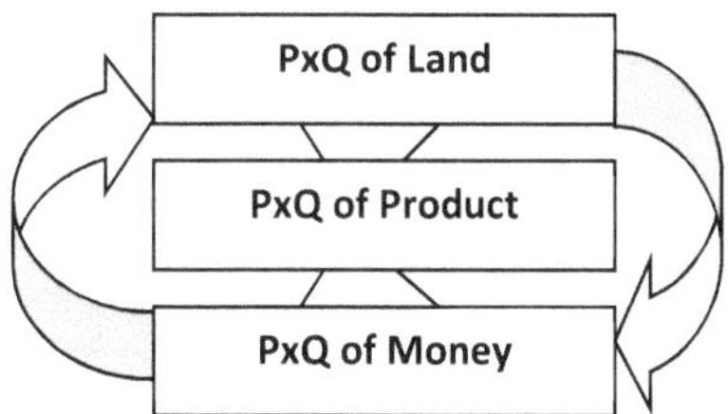

*Figure*1. A Framework of Economic Analysis

The process of price determination for the land established an equivalence (see e.g., Allen 1970, p. 748)— in conditions of equilibrium, a *constant* one to one relation— among three elements: price times quantity of land, price times quantity of product, and price times quantity of money. This process was dynamic. With the exception of the quantity of land—each specific plot of land and presumably its fertility—all the other factors were changing over time. Over time the price of the land went down, *because*—clearly—the cumulative quantity of fruit to be derived from the purchased plot of land went progressively down to zero as the 49th year approached, the year of the restitution of the land. This sliding scale method for calculating the price of the land at any given moment is evident: there was less fruit to be gathered as time progressed. Yet, what is not evident is that the economic system relied on two hidden independent relationships: the price of the fruit of the land and the value (quantity times price) of money. These relationships have to be made explicit:

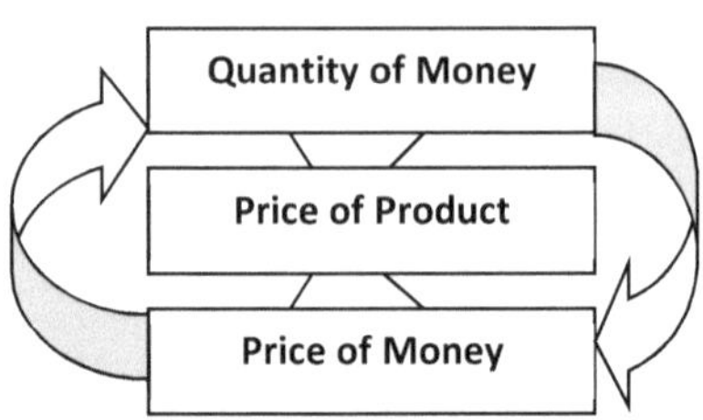

Figure 2. The Monetary Mechanism

The unit price of the fruit of the land had to remain *constant* over time; and the value of money also had to remain *constant* over time—otherwise, it would have been impossible to determine the price of a plot of land at any point in time. To wit, if the price of the fruit were to increase over time, then the price of the land could either remain constant—rather than decrease—or even increase over time. Ditto for any variation in the value of money.

We shall investigate the issue of the value of money after analyzing the legal and moral context in which the Jubilee was carried out. Here it might be worth to remain a little longer on the issue of the constancy of the price of the fruit of the land. Assume zero initial capital expenditure, constant labor costs, and no technological innovation over time, the cost of the product ought to remain *constant*. (Indeed, with technological innovation, as current market trends in computers demonstrate, in a regimen of near perfect competition the price of a product will decrease).

The Legal Context. The legal operative word is stewardship. As distinguished from "things" that we create and on which we have legitimate property rights, the land belongs neither to its possessor, nor to the government. The owner of the land is Yahweh. "The land is mine," says Yahweh (Lev 25:23). It is Yahweh who gives the land to each family of the tribes of Israel—except the Levi (Num 18:20) who were expected to live on part of the tithe (Num 18:24-30; cf. Kelly 2004). If one possessor encounters troubled economic waters, one can sell the fruit of the land. But the owner of the land remains Yahweh. And the price of the land goes down because at the Jubilee year the land goes back to the original possessor. Thus, the decreasing price makes it possible for the buyer to receive a compensation equivalent to the value of product that might be obtained until the 49th year of the Jubilee cycle. And, incidentally, it is worth noticing that it becomes less traumatic and more palatable to transfer back to the original possessor a plot of land whose residual market value goes down to zero—instead of remaining constant or increasing—as the Jubilee year approaches. (Urban houses are treated like consumer goods. They are not returned to the original owner, specifies Myron S. Geller, unless redeemed.)

The Moral Context. In Israel there was a moral obligation to return the land to the original possessor at the Jubilee year. Why this command? Why the acceptance of this command by the people—at least in the beginning? The reason is clear. The person without access to land and natural resources is not a free man or woman. This person has lost the most fundamental of God's gifts to man; he has lost his freedom. The loop is closed, the inner mechanism of the economics of Moses becomes clear as soon as it is realized—to repeat, as modern economic theory from Adam Smith onward has made clear—that freedom is an essential component of economic growth. No freedom, no wealth. Take away economic freedom from your neighbor and both you and your neighbor become poorer. Your nation becomes poorer. Thus the practice of the Jubilee concerning land does not only have internal legal and moral integrity, it makes unexceptionable and irreproachable economic sense. [Especially in olden days, access to land was an essential component of economic freedom. Concentration of the land in a few hands restricts the economic freedom existing in a nation. The injunction of the Jubilee concerning land is an essential tool of an economic policy that wants to prevent hoarding and to preserve economic freedom for the nation as a whole.] Let us now observe the inner mechanism of the Jubilee concerning money. Similarities and differences with the theory and practice of the Jubilee concerning land are quite instructive. Naturally, one reinforces the other.

The second plank of the Jubilee is the injunction that during the seventh year all personal debts (only) among the Hebrews are to be extinguished. This injunction—if ever practiced, especially outside of kinship, specifies Myron Geller—can be understood when it is inserted into a monetary framework that is dominated by these three fundamental propositions: Gold, or an equivalent commodity, is money. Debt is not money. Interest rate is zero or very near zero. To analyze these propositions, let us reconstruct the monetary framework which led the Israelites to their unique injunction. Three elements are in proportional relationship:

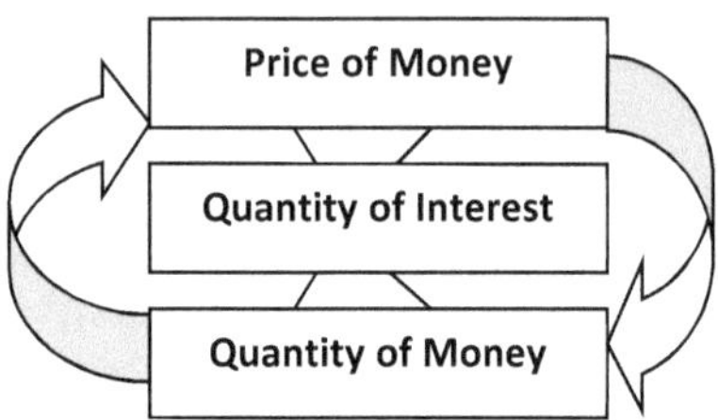

Figure 3. A Monetary Framework

In the beginning the supply of gold, being a global commodity, increased—though in spurts—at a near constant rate with the increase of the population. Hence, since its per capita utility was rather constant, the price of money was stable. The interest rate was zero (Lev 25:36-37) because the gold nugget or coin that was returned was the same as—or an equivalent to—the one borrowed; in this case the value implicit in the use of the nugget was a definite gift from the lender to the borrower. (*In the beginning,* unless other arrangements were instituted, in order to avoid paying or receiving a 100% interest rate in addition to the return of the capital, one would have had to break apart the nugget or the coin—a difficulty that was eventually obviated by issuing coins of smaller and smaller denominations. And if in time a reasonable interest rate was charged, one still remained within the bounds of the economics of the Jubilee.) *In the beginning,* money as debt did not exist. The relation between debtor and creditor remained personal and static. One did not buy or sell debt. Who would want to buy an "asset"—debt—that bears low or no interest and whose value becomes zero when the Jubilee year comes due?

But why did the value of debt become zero when the seventh year arrived? The practical reason is that the borrower had almost certainly spent the nugget or the coin borrowed and was now penniless: personal peonage did exist, but was subject to the same rules as those concerning monetary debt (see Lev 25:39-55). The cancellation of debt and the redemption from peonage renders men free again—and free human beings produce more than slaves and peons. The theoretical reason is that the cancellation of debt on the seventh year was the capstone that held an extremely delicate set of checks and balances together: the interest rate was null or very low and certainly there was no such construct as compound interest; debt had no value of its own; indeed, gold used as cash had—literally—a carrying cost and was not much subject to inflation or deflation. These relationships persisted as long as the Jubilee and Sabbatical were practiced.

Apart from the internal coherence of the system, where is the fundamental justification for the cancellation of debts during the seventh year? The case of land is clear. Yahweh creates the land; therefore, Yahweh remains its owner in perpetuity. But who creates money? Unless other textual evidence is brought forward, there is only one expression that clarifies the issue. The expression comes from Lk 20:24-25, in which Jesus, upon being shown a denarius, asked: "Whose portrait and inscription are on it?" "Caesar's," they replied. He said to them, "Then give to Caesar what is Caesar's". This is who Jesus understood to be the intermediate owner of money: Caesar; the government.

But wait. Who is the King in the Jewish tradition? What is the government? The King is anointed by Yahweh. The King and the government are representatives of Yahweh. The money, then, is as much a good that comes from Yahweh as the land. (And this, incidentally, is the foundational reason for the institution of the tithe [see Gn 14:20; Lev 27:30; and Deut 14:22]. The tithe is similar to the first fruit that in Greece or Rome and other ancient societies, and in Bali today, is given to the gods).

Thus the Jubilee/Sabbatical concerning money, the remission of all debts every seventh year, makes as much sense as the restitution of the land to the original possessor. This injunction of the Jubilee concerning money possesses just as much internal logic, as well as legal and moral integrity, as the Jubilee concerning land. The unexceptionable and irreproachable economic sense of the Jubilee concerning the land is redoubled when it assumes the form of the cancellation of debts—the cancellation of the duty to restitute wealth that no longer is there. Yet, to make the issues more deeply understood, perhaps one must ask: what is money?

Money. There is no definition of money in economic theory. And there can be none. In economic theory, there is only an explanation of the functions of money: a store of value, a means of exchange, and a tool of accounting. These, to repeat, are the functions of money. For a definition of money, one must go to the law. One can then say with certainty what money is: Money is a contract. Money is a contract between the holder of the coin—or the note—and society. It is society as a whole that gives value to the money. It is the sweat and tears of all the people that give value to money. The King, or the government, as representative of society as a whole, only vouches for its mint condition and guarantees the value of money.

Both money and land are common goods, because they are both given value by the sweat and tears of all the people in the land. A rock in Arizona is nearly worthless; a rock of the same size in Manhattan is worth gazillions. To repeat, the Jubilee does not only have internal logical, legal, and moral integrity, it makes unexceptionable and irreproachable economic sense. The practice of cancellation of debt every seventh year was an acceptance of reality and an institution of peace: one cannot spill blood from a stone. The alternative is to enslave debtors. Yet, debtors produce nothing if incarcerated—indeed, they cost money for sustenance—and slaves produce less than free men. Hence, society as a whole, just as in the case of the land, is worse off through the pursuance of sleek economic practices. These practices are generally tolerated because the cost of the sustenance of the debtor in jail is borne, not by the creditor, but by society as a whole.

This analysis is confirmed by a view of the monetary system as a whole. The monetary system has to integrate three elements: (1) a coin or a bill is to be made equivalent to (2) a unit of currency—e.g., one dollar bill; and both have to be made equivalent to (3) some amount of real wealth. This third element is shattered into an infinite number of items. The functionality of the system is ultimately determined by the (culturally always changing) exchange values among these infinite sets: one ounce of gold for one bushel of apples, and one bushel of apples for a carved walking stick, which at that one point in time must in turn be able to buy an ounce of gold. In a free economy, these exchange values are determined by the laws of supply and demand. Yet, this conclusion is much too hurried, because these exchange values are *first* determined by the number and the value of bills and coins in circulation. In other words, two thirds of monetary analysis consists of the determination of who issues the currency, conditions of issuance, and amount of currency in circulation. If the amount of currency determines the nominal value of the currency, then the essence of monetary *policy* consists of the determination of elements (1) and (2) above, namely who issues the currency and to whom is it issued—and, more specifically, the conditions under which the currency is created. To confine one's observation to the third element of the monetary process is not wrong; it is an incomplete action. It is condemning oneself to a partial view of the process: It is as if, while diligently studying all twirls, all twists and turns, of the cat, one lost track of the cat. Worse. This is not simply a theoretical conclusion. To study only the third element of the monetary process, it is not simply to abandon monetary policy to the blind forces of the market. This enclosure of vision inexorably leads to the abandonment of monetary policy either to the bankers or the politicians.

Clearly, in a duly constituted society it is not the creditor who creates the currency or its value, but the monetary authority in conjunction with the actions of the free market. The monetary authority is thus fully entitled to cancel uncollectible debts. Money is fiat money. It should not be made into a means of control over people. The monetary aspects of the Jubilee are, therefore, in full accord with a complete understanding of the monetary system as a whole.

Jubilee Concerning Products-Things-Time

One meaning of Jubilee is not just restitution, but gift. There are many sides to these injunctions: one is economic, the others are legal, social, moral, and religious; today we might add one more dimension: psychological. The Israelites are enjoined to offer gifts to the passerby, the sojourner, and the poor. A list of injunctions runs as follows: at all times, leave the corn stalk at the edge of the field untouched; leave the fruit on the lower branches of the tree untouched; leave whatever stock of grain falls from your cart so that any passerby can avail himself of this bounty—no questions asked. This proviso is all important. Its importance is made manifest not so much by the intrusive questioning of the "welfare state" of today as by the extraordinary delicacy of moral sentiments epitomized by Maimonides, the Jewish sage of the XII century Spain in which the three monotheistic religions working together, not without shortcomings, created a splendid civilization. The practice of charity—the *tzedakah*—is codified in Maimonides' "golden ladder", in which (as in the Islamic practice of *zakāh*) ultimately the line between morality and economics is overstepped and the wisdom to endow people with a business of their own is established. Why, one might ask? Because Maimonides and traditional Islamic jurists can be said to have discovered that competition is the soul of economic freedom.

The practical effects of these injunctions are multifaceted. Each injunction orders a transfer of wealth from a producer to a consumer—without any compensation, because, presumably, the passerby who avails himself of that bounty has no means to compensate the producer. The economic effect of this aspect of the Jubilee is straightforward. Consumption, as Adam Smith well knew, is "the sole end and purpose" of business: consumption completes the economic process. A penny is earned when a good is sold. If you cannot sell a product, first reduce its price—or make more money available to the consumer, as Henry Ford well knew—and then give it away This economic aspect of the Jubilee, liberally extended to cover the Sabbatical and everyday practices, should be most evident today. What board of directors will order an expansion of business when merchandise is stuck on the shelves?

The social/religious/moral/psychological effect of this aspect of the Jubilee resides in the meaning of Jubilee as freedom: freedom from attachment to products, attachment to things— which we create and on which we have proper property rights. And to the list of attachments, today, one must add time. We are so attached to our freedom to do whatever we please with our time that we neglect to offer it, at least every seventh day, to our families and our communities—and ultimately to ourselves and preferably to God. How can the wisdom of the practice of the Sabbath have slid from our hands so irresponsibly? Perhaps it will help us to understand, if we decipher Pharaoh's message contained in Ex 5:9 along such explicit lines as: "Let us so overwork the people that they will be incapable of listening to words of truth". And of course the core of the Jewish message is that Yahweh grants us freedom to worship him without fear all the days of our life—a freedom that clearly extends to the choice not to worship him.

[The guess is that we have not considered the many implications of free time. Perhaps it will help us to understand, if we decipher Pharaoh's message contained in Ex 5:9 along such explicit lines as: "Let us so overwork the people that they will be incapable of listening to words of truth." Perhaps it will help us to understand the need to abstain from work on the Sabbath day, if we consider the relationships between free time and all the work that needs to be done in order to insure one's economic freedom: One needs to insure the health of one's own physical body; one needs to insure the health of political body of the nation. One needs to think. One needs to have the time to get out of one's own limited shell. And of course the core of the Jewish message is that Yahweh grants us freedom to worship him without fear all the days of our life—a freedom that clearly extends to the choice not to worship him.]

Only a saint could have understood the deepest possible aspects of the detachment from products, things, and even time. Saint Catherine of Siena says (1980, p. 322): "(Those who are detached from things) do not fear the bitterness of death." The right relation with products, things, and time grants the greatest freedom of all: freedom from fear of dying—a fear experienced a thousand times by many a person who is abnormally attached to things. If in doubt, Google "hoarding" and be amazed at the findings.

2. Do Not Steal

Seen in the total complexity of the economic aspects of the Jubilee, the second doctrine of the economics of Moses—a well-known doctrine—ought to acquire its original full force: *Do Not Steal*. Do not steal money and do not steal land, it is clear, because they do not belong to you, or even to their possessors. They are common goods. Ultimately they both belong to Yahweh. If you steal land or money, you offend Yahweh—directly.

The injunction against stealing extends to consumer goods as well. And here the legal and moral foundation of the injunction is as strong as it can possibly be. In a primitive society, there is no mystery as to the origin of consumer goods. They issue directly from the sweat and tears of people. Hence, these goods belong to those who

31

have created them. More. In a primitive society in which consumer goods are not only few but essential to life, stealing them is tantamount to killing other people.

Does one dare ask the quintessential moral-practical question: Is it all any different today? Are there not people starving—even starving to death—today?

This, of course, is a paper devoted to economics. Where is the economic rationale for the injunction against stealing? The forms of stealing are legion; and so are the costs of stealing. Unjustly dispossessed people are less productive than people who are secure in their possessions. Indeed, stealing is the ultimate form of corruption. Economics is just beginning to appreciate the costs of corruption in the business world—both within developed and developing countries. Would any financial crisis be as severe, if there were no corruption in high places?

***

A Preliminary Evaluation. The extremely delicate sets of checks and balances composing the economics of Moses doomed it to a relatively short life. As soon as either greed became unbridled or the theological bonds were loosened, the system could no longer work. But while it worked, what a system it was; what a beacon to the ages. It was the creation of a perfectly just economy. Israel must have indeed been so rich as to attract the envy of its neighbors, even so often to become the object of conquest and plunder

A Question. People ask: Was the Jubilee really practiced? An imprecise answer is that the Jubilee was practiced with a decreasing intensity from—before?—the time of Moses to the time of Jesus, and that the legal mantel of stewardship covering land and money worked, and worked quite well for society as a whole. Hence, a more precise answer: The Jubilee was practiced as long as the people of Israel remained free. And that is the rub! The absence of chicanery and theft coupled with the practice of the Jubilee, the return of the land to the original possessors and the cancellation of debts after so many years, restored the inner balance of the economic relationships in Israel. There were no poor (Deut 15:4), or very few poor people.

Investment occurred naturally—so much so that Moses did not need to speak of investment.

Would the Economics of Moses Have Been Practiced in a Non-Theocratic Society? The answer is an undiluted, Yes. The economics of Moses has been practiced since time immemorial, and still is being practiced: in the commons, until they are enclosed. (A WORTHY PAUSE. *Private ownership tends to be absolute. It wants to enclose the commons, against the Bible's injunction never to sell the commons [Lev 25:34]; even at the cost of the demise of the enclosed commons—as Hardin well knew. This is the chain reaction: monetization of the enclosures leads to overcapitalization because initial expenditures of money must be recovered at a profit and on time; overcapitalization leads to overexploitation and speculation, which lead to financial and natural collapse. There has never been a collapse of the commons; there has always and everywhere been a collapse of the enclosures.*) The size of the economy is not the issue, either. The economics of Moses was practiced by the American Indians over the vast prairies when they were free.

The substance of the economics of Moses can be summarized simply. Morality creates freedom; and freedom creates wealth. The freedom of wealth acquired in justice ultimately produces jubilation in the heart. That is the ultimate aim of the economics of Moses.

Now is the time to go from the economics of Moses to the economics of Jesus in order to discern more clearly the relationship between economic freedom and investment.

Part II — The Economics of Jesus

Three doctrines comprise the economics of Jesus: *Invest Your Talents; Do Not Hoard Your Talents; Give to Caesar What Is Caesar's.*

1. Invest Your Talents

From Moses to Jesus Investing as the Normal Outcome of Economic Freedom

The word "investment" had not been invented yet, but the practice was there from time immemorial—if not from the first appearance of men and women on earth. And so was the intellectual understanding that this practice revolves around three factors of production: land, capital, and labor. We have observed how Israel intellectually handled both money and land from Moses to Jesus. Why is labor not an essential component of the economics of Moses?

In the beginning there was work, but no "labor." Every member of the tribes of Israel received a plot of land for his own use, except the Levi who were to live on 1/10 of the tithe. Therefore, **everyone was an owner**, *not a worker or a laborer*— and the practice of the Jubilee tended to reinforce this status. Hence there was economic freedom in the land. From Moses to Jesus investing was such a normal outcome of economic freedom that Moses did not have to speak of investing at all. By the time of Jesus, evidently much economic freedom had already been eroded. The Jubilee was no longer practiced. Indeed, with the Roman conquest the Mosaic mantel of stewardship over land and money was captured by the Roman institution of private property. Acquisition was in the saddle. Most people lost possession of their land and debts impoverished them even faster. Some people became laborers. Jesus has a forceful account of the condition of labor. Mt 20:8-15 gives this parable of the workers in the vineyard who at the end of the day …lined up to receive their pay. The ones hired last were paid first. Having worked but an hour, they didn't expect much. To their surprise and delight, however, they each received a full denarius. When the workers who were hired first saw this, they—forgetting their bargain—became happily expectant. If that was what the employer was paying to those who had worked but a single hour, then how much more would they have coming! So they thought. When they received their own pay, however, it was but one denarius, like the others. Their fallen expectation turned to bitterness, and they confronted the employer, saying: "These last have wrought but one hour, yet thou hast made them equal to us, who have bourne the burden and the heat of the entire day." The employer, however, was not impressed. To one of them, he replied: "Friend, I am not being unfair to you. Didn't you agree to work for a denarius? Take your pay and go. I want to give this man who was hired last the same as I gave you. Don't I have the right to do what I want with my own money? Or are you envious because I am generous?"

As all parables, this too has received a myriad of interpretations. The present context suggests this meaning. This is what Jesus seems to say: "Yahweh gave you possession of the land; Moses gave you the Jubilee to correct your possible economic mistakes. If you tolerate a system in which there is no Jubilee or any of its equivalents, you have no economic freedom. You have a system of masters and slaves. And, legally as well as theologically, you cannot tell the master what to do. You can cry to high haven, but not even God is going to listen to you. Either you regain your God-given economic freedom, whereby you yourself (in concord with other co-owners if you have any) have the right to reward your endeavors in accordance with what you think is just, or you simply have to accept what the master decides to give you—no matter how arbitrary; no matter how unjust; no matter, even, how generous that reward is."

This is the condition that still prevails. That is why, for instance, all attempts to establish a "living wage" are destined to fail—no matter how well-intentioned, no matter how persistently pursued. Outside the institution of ownership of land, of capital, and of one's own labor, there is no way of accounting what is just or unjust— or even logical. As Franco Modigliani (1980, p. xiv) frankly admitted, there is "no rigorous analysis" of "the mechanism determining wages and prices…. Indeed, the modeling of wage behavior remains to this day the Achilles heel of macroeconomic analysis." The shortcut is, and will forever be, to treat labor as a commodity.

Are we left by Jesus forever without recourse against intrinsic injustices of the "wage contract? Not at all. As Jesus implied, to redress injustices, the labor movement has to transform itself into the ownership or equity movement—with union dues attached, not to wages, but to ownership shares. The list of inalienable rights of workers will never become full enough to yield a satisfactory solution to the "labor question"; this list must be transformed into a single item: the right to own the fruits created by one's labor—a right that has to cover capital appreciation.

Jesus thus emphasizes what Moses implied and what every Classical economist was later (almost) to emphasize: Take proper care of (the ownership of) land, capital, and labor and economic growth will result as a normal outcome of economic freedom. Yet, were we to leave the issue at that we would be making a grievous mistake. We would be neglecting the historical context and, consequently, we would not foster a true understanding of the economics of Jesus.

From Moses to Adam Smith Investing Is Done in Accordance with the Moral Law

 As there are many planks in the economics of Moses that need to be made explicit, so there is one essential corollary of the doctrine of Jesus regarding investment that must be brought forward: From Moses to Adam Smith, everyone agreed that economic life is covered by the moral law. The understanding of this complex interlacing of moral and economic injunctions was held astonishingly constant over time. This view, confirms Wood (2002, p. 83), was "the same as Aristotle's". It is only from Adam Smith onward that there has been a breach in this tradition. (Free marketers assume that this reality still prevails—and, in a fundamental way, they are right.)

Modern economics, it is widely maintained, is a science—indeed, a mathematical and an autonomous science. As such, economics is supposed to be studied by itself and, certainly, its internal cohesion precludes the examination of any external consideration; especially any consideration regarding morality. These statements, by themselves, are inarguable. Yet, as most people sense, they are fallacious. Their fallacy is revealed only realizing that they do not stand alone but are part of an intellectual system whose fundamental propositions are as follows:

1. Freedom $\rightarrow \infty$
2. Morality $\rightarrow 0$
3. (Monetary) Efficiency $= 1$ (sole value)
4. Economic agents $= ||$ (isolated logical automatons)
5. Community $\rightarrow 0$.

In Appendix A we shall demonstrate that not one of these propositions stands at the touch of reason. For the time being, suffice to notice that the conflict between morality and economics is not a postulate of modern economics; the moral consequences of economics are immaterial to economists. Therefore, the separation of morality from economics can be considered as a transient phenomenon, a transient aberration that time will allow us to forget. We will then discover that Adam's Fallacy (Foley 2006), with all its rationalizations, has gone away by blinking it away. Here we can only distil the extended analysis into the following proposition: Human beings are free—not to choose between Gucci and Pucci—but between good and evil.

Let us parse this sentence. Economic growth is not a monotonic function of freedom. There are two forces that move human life and, by definition, the economic system: one is freedom, the other is morality. Jesus was very specific as to what he meant by morality. He did not fall into the trap of determining for others what is good or evil. Jesus did not make this severe strategic error. As outstanding proofs, he did not suggest any external restriction on economic activity or any forcible transfer of wealth from one group of people to another. Hence, he would concur that economic activity must be free and he would add that morality cannot be imposed—or slapped on—from the outside, because then morality becomes empty of content. Either morality is within each and every decision that one takes or it is not there at all. Thus Jesus made it very clear that he wanted morality to be applied ever creatively. He wanted moral rules to be forever internalized. And easily memorized. He reduced the whole of morality in economics to two economic doctrines: *Do not Hoard; Give to Caesar What Is Caesar's.*

2. Do Not Hoard

The freedom to choose between Gucci and Pucci is not an economic decision. It is an esthetic decision. The economic decision is whether to spend one's income and wealth on consumer and capital goods or to hoard it. Analysis shows that this choice is more than a simple economic decision; it is an intrinsically moral decision with clearly identifiable economic consequences. Jesus was extraordinarily firm about this choice, which—since reasonable people are assumed to buy consumer goods only as they need them and moral people are supposed to know how to choose between buying *another* Gucci bag or giving the money to the neighbor who is starving—he characteristically reduced it to the choice between investing and hoarding. In the Parable of the Talents as written in Mt 25:14-30, Jesus so forcefully applauded using wealth creatively that all the wealth was donated to those who had doubled it—and they were enthusiastically entrusted with the administration of much more wealth. Clearly, Jesus applauded investing so because moral people are supposed to know the difference between producing a Gucci bag or a loaf of bread. By the same token, Jesus so strongly condemned hoarding as to take the one talent away from the person who, for fear of losing it, planted it underground where it could do no good for anyone. Much more. This person was ordered to be cast into hell, literally "the outer darkness; (w)here men will weep and gnash their teeth". No appeal. No mercy.

Only understanding the economic consequences of hoarding does one see that Jesus was fully justified in such an uncharacteristically strong and uncharitable position. Those who doubt the relevance of hoarding in relation to the modern economy might want to read Appendix B first. Or they might want to fast forward (which in actual time is fast backward) to reading *The Economic Process.* There they will discover that hoarding is the hidden-to-economists bottleneck that strangles economic growth (235-70); that hoarding is the hidden-to-economists seed of inflation (271-302); that hoarding has the hidden-to-economists property of being in a one-to-one relationship with the level of poverty (329-53). Without the need for too much elaboration, readers will also discover that, through the transmission belt of economic rights and responsibilities, the elimination of hoarding is ultimately the spring of Economic Liberty, Economic Freedom and Economic Justice for all (355-58).

Should anyone wonder that Jesus was such a superb economist and political scientist? Well, those who might want to confine Jesus to the straightjacket of theology, will have to admit that Jesus' doctrine of not hoarding becomes clearer if, first and foremost, it is seen as an explicit formulation—and an extension—of the clear and compelling Mosaic Law of the Jubilee, the clear-as-a-bell and compelling-as-a-knocker Mosaic Law of the Jubilee.

Do Not Hoard in the Mosaic Law

As expressed in the Jewish Law, the injunction against hoarding is presented as a list of positive activities, which in a decreasing order of importance can be enumerated as follows: return the land to the original possessor every forty-nine years; cancel all existing debts every seven years; let the land lie fallow every seven years; reserve the Sabbath, the seventh day of the week, for God and community, for family, and for yourself; leave the corn stalk at the hedge of the field untouched;

leave the fruit on the lower branches of the tree untouched; leave whatever stock of grain falls from your cart so that any passerby can avail himself of this bounty—no questions asked, no compensation required.

Jesus synthesized the list of positive actions prescribed by the Mosaic law and the Jewish prophets into a negative injunction: do not hoard. Thus he generalized and extended the original formulation of this injunction, by including in it all forms of hoarding. This formulation has a set of explicatory characteristics of its own. In it, the economic—as distinguished from the theocratic and moral—aspects of the Jubilee become exceedingly transparent. The fundamental reason why at the appointed years the land had to be returned to the original tiller and debts had to be cancelled was to prevent hoarding: the inordinate accumulation of wealth in the hands of the few—and the consequent deprivation for the many of the means of sustenance. With the amount of wealth being finite at any particular moment, when the few have too much, the many have too little. (Technically, wealth hoarded is only wealth that is used neither as a consumer good nor as a capital good. The land ordered back to the original possessor might not have all been hoarded. Yet, most of it was—as the existence of much unused land indicated.) The Prophet Mohammed put it most simply and clearly: "Let him who owns land cultivate it himself, and if he does not do so let him have his brother cultivate it" (Chapra, 1985, p. 85). The Arapaho American Indians put this commandment this way: "Take only what you need and leave the land as you found it" (Zona, 1994, p. 88).

Jesus was very clear as to this relationship. For him cause and effect was so immediate that he emphasized in no uncertain terms the destination of the wealth not to be hoarded: It ought to be given to the poor. He felt so strongly about the issue that he personalized it. He said in Mt 25:40: "whatever you did for one of the least of these brothers of mine, you did for me."

Why did Jesus emphasize so forcefully the need of giving to the poor? Generally, this injunction is characterized as being a moral injunction. And that is certainly true; but it is not a sufficient interpretation of Jesus' position. It is the economic content of this injunction that links the economics of Moses to the economics of Jesus and gives substance to the moral injunction of giving to the poor: giving to the poor not just a pittance, but giving them what is their due. We have so far seen that the Israelites—let alone the rest of the world—by not practicing any of the forms of the Jubilee had gradually lost their original economic freedom. And the number of poor people was growing at an intolerable pace. Certainly, there were many more poor people at the time of Jesus than at the time of Moses. But this is a historical fact that does not explain much; indeed, it is a trend that needs to be explained. A major institutional change occurred from the time of Moses to the time of Jesus. Hebrew stewardship of land and money was transformed into Roman private ownership of land and money: land and money were privatized. These common goods could then be accumulated beyond the requirement of the satisfaction of one's needs. The latifundia—those exceedingly large estates that still plague the world today—were born; and the insidious accumulation of financial resources was beginning to be felt in the economic system. A part of these resources was accumulated and kept idle—all the while people were excluded from their utilization and were made poor as a consequence. With the latifundia came poverty.

This, then, is the first essential characteristics of Jesus' doctrine of not hoarding. By turning his own negative into a positive injunction, the doctrine acquires an economic content that does not stand in a vacuum but is immediately related to the rest of society. The poor are poor not because the rich are rich nor because the rich are the creators of poverty (cf. Gorga, 1998)—Jesus had nothing against the rich. The poor are poor because the rich have too much, too much they do not need. The second essential characteristic of Jesus' doctrine of not hoarding is this. It places the primary responsibility for not hoarding, implicitly on society and the law, but explicitly on individual conscience. Hoarding clearly becomes a moral issue with distinct economic consequences. Dishoarding becomes a voluntary act. Jesus wanted each one of us to be convinced of the importance of our own rights and responsibilities and to act upon them. Jesus did not start an economic movement. The third essential characteristic of Jesus' doctrine of not hoarding is this: Do not wait forty-nine years before divesting yourself of unneeded wealth. The time to dishoard is now. And with this he exalted the value of practices recommended in Mosaic and rabbinic law.

Hoarding from Jesus to Locke

It seems that from Jesus to Locke (1698, esp. Bk. II, Ch. V, pars. 46-51) everyone knew about hoarding and the need to give to the poor. St. John Chrysostom (347-407), concerned with how to give to the poor, exploded (Tierney, 1959, p. 55): "Let us have no more of this ridiculous, diabolical, peremptory prying" into the lives of people who ask for assistance. With various dissenting opinions, the Catholic

Church from its beginning up until the age of Adam Smith maintained that surplus wealth of the rich legally belonged to the poor (*ibid.* esp. pp. 22-44).

Thus the moral injunction of giving to the poor was transformed into a strict—however imperfectly practiced—legal injunction: the surplus of one's wealth, whatever one—on the basis of one's own independent counsel—did not need, belonged do the poor (*ibid.* esp. p. 106). The poor took the place of the original owner of the Jewish Law of the Jubilee. The penalty was excommunication. The same was true in relation to usury, which in its simplest formulation can be defined as the request of exorbitant rates of interest. Usury, the fastest method for people to grow rich at the expense of others who need to borrow money, was consistently discouraged from Jesus to Locke.

Islamic law against usury is the only stronghold left against hoarding in the modern world and it has given rise to innovative practices that range from microfinancing to equity-financing.

Why? Why this disappearance of the concern for hoarding in the modern world? The answer to this puzzle is extraordinarily simple. The disappearance of the concern for hoarding has occurred because the practice of hoarding goes undetected in modern economic theory.

The Disappearance of Hoarding in Modern Economic Theory Since Adam Smith

Enter Adam Smith into the field of economics and the memory of three thousand years of history is erased from our consciousness. Hoarding disappears from sight. Not for naught Adam Smith is considered the father of modern economics. Today, economists can no longer see hoarding. Economists may even talk about hoarding, but formally—mathematically and logically—hoarding, as is well known, cannot enter into even the most minute interstices of modern economic theory. All income that is not spent on consumer goods is assumed to be saved and all saving is assumed to be "equal" to investment: there is no room for hoarding. Hoarding disappeared from the purview of economic theory when Adam Smith, being no economist but a professor of moral philosophy, unawares conflated two conflicting categories of thought, two irreconcilable phenomena—hoarding and investment (capital)—into one: accumulation. Worse still. Adam Smith saw a distinction between saving and investment (1776, Bk. II., Ch. 3, pars. 14-18) that, since it is nowhere to be found in economic reality, has in vain been searched for in economic theory. Not for naught the relationship between saving and investment is officially classified as a quagmire. In fact, the distinction between saving and investment is only a differentiation between two degrees of risk—hence, two different degrees of potential income stream. There is no conceptual, no purely economic distinction between saving and investment.

Damn the reality. Damn sound economic reasoning. Damn economic theory. Full speed ahead. When Adam Smith entered the field of economics, saving took the place of hoarding. Hoarding was relegated to the past (1776, Bk. V., Ch. 3, pars. 1, 2, 9) and disappeared from sight.

Worse, much worse things were to follow. Since he had no understanding of the morality of economics and—pity for a professor of moral philosophy (and a deist)— he had an ax to grind against the morality of the monks (see esp. 1776, B. V. Ch. 1, par. 158), Adam Smith preached the doctrine of "accumulation of riches" (see esp. 1776, B. II, Ch. 3, par. 35).

At that moment, losing its moorings in morality, economics lost its rudder and sense of direction. It became a mechanistic discipline. Under the guidance of modern economic theory, the economic system is assumed to be ruled, not by human decisions, but by "the blind forces of the market." Man is out of the saddle. Man is assumed to be an innocent bystander.

A Modern Chorus of Approval

Having lost the memory of the past, most economists stand ready to proclaim the inevitability of the present. At this juncture in the conversation, joining their voices to a chorus of free-marketers (who assume that morality is practiced, as it is practiced, by all self-respecting economic agents) and winner-take-all analysts who study the economics of gambling and Hollywood stardom, most economists are likely to pitch in and say: "The forces of the market, rather than justifying the economics of Moses and Jesus, prove that wealth accumulation—which is not recognized as being, in part, hoarding—is 'natural' and 'inevitable'. After all, did not Jesus, in Mt 26:11, quoting Deut 15:11, say, 'The poor will always be with you'"? These analysts have not factored in their analysis the distinction between hoarding ex post and hoarding ex ante. In so doing, they let the mechanics of hoarding pass under their radar undetected. Jesus was concerned with both stages of hoarding. He did not only say "Do Not Hoard" and, if you happened to have hoarded in the past, "Dishoard Now". Perhaps he was even more concerned with preventing hoarding from happening at all. He went after hoarding at its roots. He also said: "Give to Caesar What Is Caesar's." The evidence is strong that inordinate accumulation of wealth is due to the contravention of this last doctrine.

3. Give to Caesar What Is Caesar's

The third economic doctrine of Jesus, *Give to Caesar What Is Caesar's*, has traditionally been interpreted too narrowly. Betraying their intellectual roots in the work of Consultant Administrators from the fifteenth century Italy, modern economists have limited the application of this doctrine to the relationship between government and the governed. Thus, having abandoned monetary policy into the hands of the bankers, modern economists have not only reduced economic policy to fiscalism; more seriously still, they have restricted the vision of the economics of Jesus to a master/servant relationship. To understand the full import of the third economic doctrine of Jesus, we need to enlarge its range of applicability by enveloping the entire gamut of relations that exist among free men and women. Once one observes the whole economic process, as Classical economists did and as Keynes or Hayek did, then the third economic doctrine of Jesus reveals its not surprising complexity. The third doctrine then reads as follows: give the other fellow what is his due. This, as it has been known from Aristotle onward, is the very essence of economic justice. Once that is done, we shall see that giving to Caesar what is Caesar's is nothing but the application of Moses Law: Do not steal. Jesus did not present any new proposition in Jewish Law. He simply transformed a negative Mosaic commandment, "Do not steal", into a positive injunction: "Do Justice". Thus he followed Deut 16:20.

Let us leave petty larceny well alone. To put substance into this third doctrine, let us realize that when people do not pay the full share of the taxes they owe, especially taxes on land and natural resources, they steal from fellow citizens who are burdened with the total share of the costs of running a country. When the central bank sells the national credit to preferred customers, the central bank sells for a mess of pottage a national treasure that belongs to the entire population. Private appropriation of common goods—such as land and money—without compensation is expropriation and plunder. When stockholders cash in the value of their stocks and bonds, they rob the workers who have originally contributed to the creation of

43

that value—and are excluded from that bounty by the faulty legal institute of "wage contract". When one purchases a whole corporation, and uses other people's money to concentrate the wealth of the nation into fewer and fewer hands, one robs at least the workers, if not also the previous as well as future potential stockholders, of the ensuing capital appreciation of the corporation.

Set these four economic mechanisms of capital accumulation aright, and hoarding is cut at its root. You will Give to Caesar What Is Caesar's. You will do justice and receive justice. With a just distribution of wealth, there is no need for its redistribution. Indeed, you will implement the spirit of Moses' Jubilee. Clearly, Jesus not only explicitly called for the application of Moses' Jubilee (esp. Lk 4:16-32 read with the help of Trocmé 1973, pp. 26-29); to preserve their spirit, he changed the form of Moses' injunctions and adapted them to the needs of the moment.

Some Effects of the Economics of Moses and the Economics of Jesus

The economy that invests its talents; the economy that does not hoard; the economy that gives to each his due is a full participant in the economics of Moses and Jesus—a set of doctrines whose central tenets, a preliminary investigation reveals, are shared by virtually all religious systems. This is an economy in which agents are neither automatons nor abstractions, but fully integrated persons composed of body, mind, and soul (does one prefer "character" as the free integrative factor between mind and body?); men and women who—endowed with a full complement of virtues and vices—are confronting fundamental questions at every step in their journey, because economics is not the result of blind forces; the economic process is the result of simple and clear choices. This is an economy in which both secular and religious leaders feel the responsibility to suggest that men and women should follow the virtues rather than their vices—for their immediate and ultimate good, as well as for the good of everyone else. This is an economy in which costs are fully accounted for; real costs, not accounting fictions pursued through the subterfuge of externalities or by shifting costs of living onto the shoulders of the community. This is an economy in which the land, rather than being forced to produce more than it can, rather than being treated as a source of exploitation and a dumping ground, is treated as sacred. Hence the world is unencumbered of the threat of ecological disaster. This is an economy in which life is not reduced to money. This is an economy that exists in real time and produces real goods and services. In such an economy, efficiency cannot be separated from morality; rather, efficiency is a result of morality. This proposition bears repeating: Efficiency is the result of morality. This is an economy in which one does not only demand to receive economic justice at the hand of others; one extends economic justice to all others. This is an economy that runs to the tune of justice. This is an economy functioning within a just society. The result of the economics of Moses and Jesus is peace and concord. Economics, properly professed, does not lead to strife; it is not made for man-wolf or for man-savage, as in the Hobbesian and Rousseauan abstractions, which lacked any understanding of economics and yet remain the dominating features in our spectrum of political considerations. Economics, properly professed, does not lead to begging, as we are all compelled to do these days. (Do not the rich beg for lower taxes? The middle classes for jobs? And the poor for entitlements?) The result of the economics of Moses and Jesus is not the frantic economy. The result of the economics of Moses and Jesus is serenity. And it is on the bedrock of serenity that a deep appreciation for life develops. Hence the economics of Moses, the economics of Jesus ultimately leads to the economics of jubilation—in the end, jubilation for the presence of Yahweh, giver of all the bounties of life. For Moses and Jesus, life is whole.

Where is the Evidence?

Where is the evidence, the reader might ask, that these are indeed the effects of the implementation of the economics of Moses and the economics of Jesus? The evidence lies in the economy of Zion in which the economics of Moses was implemented and in the economy of the Middle Ages in which the economics of Jesus was implemented. That Zion was the land of "milk and honey" (Ex 3:8) or that manna came down from heaven (Ex 16; Num 11:6-9; Ps 77:24-25; Wis 16:20) or that Moses struck the rock at Meriba twice to produce water—rather than simply praying for it, and was punished for his lack of faith—(Num 20:2-13) is not admissible evidence. Nor can one take historical accounts composed by Doctors of the Catholic Church as unbiased evidence. Reliable evidence, however, can be found elsewhere. The effects of the economics of Moses and the economics of Jesus have been studied by some of the most rabid adversaries of the Catholic Church; one might even call some of them enemies of Western civilization. These can be relied upon. Hence, for the effects of the implementation of the economics of Moses, the reader is invited to peruse the vast literature on the economy of the American Indians as they existed before the arrival of Columbus in Hispaniola, before

Giovanni Caboto (an ancestor of the Cabots) reached the shores of New England, and before Sir Ferdinando Gorges (one of this writer's ancestors) became Proprietor of Maine. For the effects of the implementation of the economics of Jesus, the reader is invited to pore over paintings of Pieter Bruegel the Elder or Ambrogio Lorenzetti. The cultural background of Lorenzetti's *Allegory of Good Government* is not Judeo-Christian but classical antiquity. For good measure, the fresco is located not in a church, but in Palazzo Pubblico (City Hall) of Siena.

A Personal Question and a Personal Answer

A personal question is often asked of a writer who writes along the lines written above: "Would you prefer to live in the economy of the Middle Ages?" A short personal answer is "No". A more extended one can be framed along these lines. No human institution is perfect. No period in history has been perfect. Nor will it ever be. The only issue is, can we do better today? If the response to this question is positive, then it behooves us to inquire how can we implement the tenets of the economics of Moses and the economics of Jesus in the full splendor and the full complexity of a modern economy. This is our next task, an essential task.

Part III — An Update

Within the economics of Moses and the economics of Jesus, wealth is not an end; wealth is a tool. Economics is not about money; economics is all about relationships among human beings. The goal of economics is not to become rich; it is to live— like human beings, in peace and justice, and in a state of jubilation. Modern economics, instead, seems to lead only to grumbling (cf. Ex 16:1-12). No matter how much we have, we never have enough. If the difference between modern economics and the economics of Moses and Jesus is so stark, is there any way of bridging the gap and investing our ancestral principles into the modern world? The economic Jubilee has not been practiced for millennia and, apart from the realm of Islamic law, policy restraints against hoarding have not been discussed, let alone practiced, for centuries. Is it even conceivable to insert the economics of Moses and Jesus into the modern world? The answer is rather simple and direct. To fit the economics of Moses and Jesus into the modern world, one must update economic theory; one must formulate a just economic policy; and one must start practicing what one preaches. We need to change, not our nature, but our social structures.

Updating Economic Theory

Contrary to likely expectations, it is modern economic theory that needs to be updated. Economic theory, as is widely recognized, is in a state of crisis. Indeed, it has been in a state of crisis at least since the publication in 1936 of Keynes' *General Theory*, the foundational work of modern economic theory. Following the recommendation of Keynes himself (1973, esp. pp. 47 and 150) or the recommendation of Friedrick Hayek ([1963]1995, p. 49 and 1994, p. 145), if one wants to solve the crisis in modern economic theory, one had better go back to the General Theory. And yet, once there, one is faced with a work that has often been described as wholly or in part "obscure" (see, e.g., Samuelson, 1946).

The reader will not be surprised to learn that the source of the deep avowed intellectual difficulties Keynes experienced in writing the General Theory (e.g., 1936, p. viii) resides in his unexamined acceptance of Adam Smith's conception of saving (Gorga 2002, pp. 79-92). In a hurry to solve the impossible intellectual problem of converting saving into investment, since saving is already an investment, by illegitimately equating the two Adam Smith spun the study of economics off a tangent into a world of shattered intellectualism in which, as Keynes (1936, p. 292) put it, "nothing is clear and everything is possible"; this is a world in which, as R. W. Goldsmith (1955-1956, p. 69n) calculated, saving assumes 100,000 logical meanings.

What is to be done? One needs to restrict the word saving to the world of finance. One then blinks away the silent revolution—the unheralded and undetected revolution—brought by Adam Smith to economics. By so doing, nothing is lost but confusion. All technical skills and all valid knowledge that have been acquired in the meantime are still there. Restoration can begin.

With room again available for the millennial conception of hoarding, formal changes in the General Theory (Gorga 2002, pp. 93-118, 139- 58) lead to this proposition:

$$\text{Investment} = \text{Income} - \text{Hoarding}.$$

Three thousand years of history reappear to view. In fact, upon reflection, it can be seen that this statement contains nothing but the mathematical formulation of the Parable of the Talents. In this formulation is the seed of the mathematization of the economics of Jesus and the economics of Moses. The laborious logico-mathematical steps in this process (Gorga 2002, pp. 41-158) can be eschewed thanks to the assistance of geometry; only the results of these elaborations are given in Appendix C. The fundamental equation of the economics of Jesus can be represented by a Lorenz diagram in which Time is put on the horizontal axis and the Quantity of both investment (I) and hoarding (H) on the vertical axis:

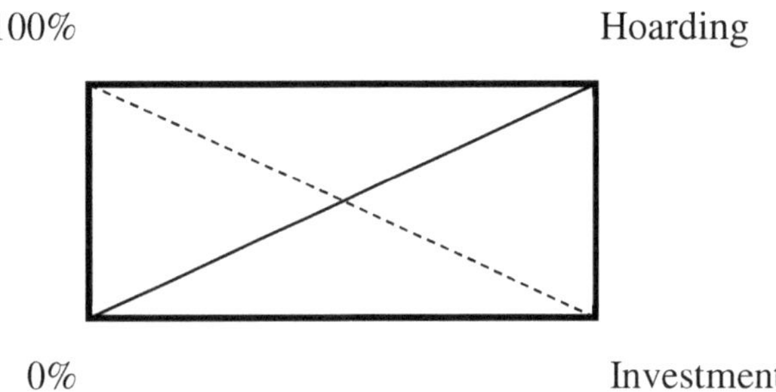

Figure 4. The Investment-Hoarding Nexus

Of course, this is a stylized representation of reality. Actual figures would produce much more erratic patterns, but the message is clear. At any one instant, the more investment, the less hoarding—and vice versa. The more real investment, the more growth of real goods and services. Hence, hoarding becomes visible as the determining factor of economic growth. This consequence is axiomatic. A little less evident is the discovery of the second major economic effect of hoarding: Hoarding is the determining factor of poverty. If, given appropriate economic policies, the more goods and services, the lower the levels of poverty in a nation; then, hoarding by the few creates artificial scarcity; it creates impossibility of investment by the many—and many fall so far behind as to become poor, to not be able to afford the basic necessities of life.

In figure 4, then, we find the essential elements of the aggregate supply function. As Brady (2004a, 2004b, and 2006) demonstrates, this function—and the aggregate demand function—is fully specified in the General Theory. The game "what Keynes really said" is over.

In our presentation, the aggregate demand function can be made visible by duplicating figure 4 and reading it solely in monetary terms. Through this process we basically separate the monetary economy from the real economy. Then, since there must be a relationship between these two components of the economic world, we search for a third element to link them together and we find it in the set of rules and regulations that in every society governs the distribution of ownership rights over real and monetary wealth—and we do not stray away from pure economic theory, because we are presented with the monetary value of those rights. Hence, we are given a new national accounting system. Analytical models—of stocks as well as flows—of real and monetary wealth can be found in Gorga (1982; 1991a; and 2002, pp. 25, 38, 156, 308-319).

Diagrammatically, this integration can be represented in this fashion:

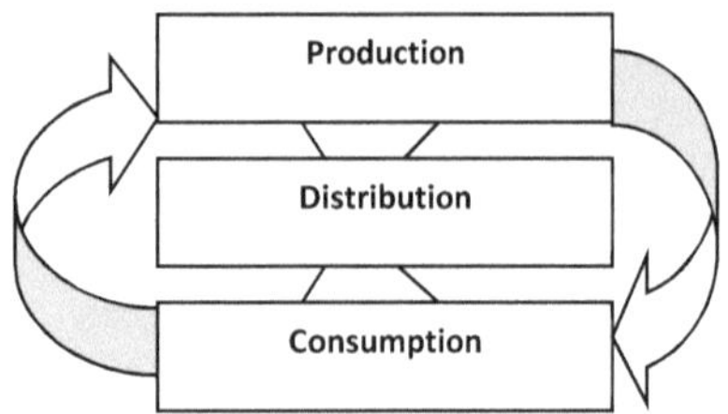

Figure 5. The Economic Process

Figure 5 reads as follows. When real goods and services pass from producers to consumers, monetary instruments of an equivalent value pass from consumers to producers. Then, one cycle of the economic process is completed—and is accompanied by the silent exchange of values of ownership rights over monetary and real wealth. Both money and goods change hands. The unit of account can be the economy of one person, one city, one nation, or the world as a whole. In macroeconomics, the exchange occurs neither between two insignificant commodities (cf. Schumpeter 1936) as in microeconomics nor between any two forms of financial instruments as in the economics of Wall Street. In macroeconomics, the total production of goods and services is exchanged for the total availability of financial resources—as in Keynes' principle of effective demand. The exchange of course occurs on the basis of relative prices as well as within the confines of a regimen of social and legal relationships, as best emphasized by the total opus of Friedrick Hayek.

One of the merits of figure 5 is that it describes the economic process as a whole. Everything is instantaneously related to everything else. Thus we bring the mathematics and geometry of economics up to the standards that prevail among engineers and scientists (see, e.g., Thompson 1986, p.36). We run away from the shattered world of the schools and go back to the world of Classical economists who knew that economics is composed of the integration of Production, Distribution, and Consumption of wealth. This integration can be made more specific by a more extensive reading of the terms, along these lines: Production is production of real goods and services (as studied especially by Supply-Side economists); Distribution is distribution of the value of ownership rights over real and monetary wealth (as studied especially by Institutionalists); Consumption is consumption—or expenditure—of monetary, i.e. financial instruments (as studied especially by Demand-Side economists).

Figure 5 depicts the economic process at one instant in time. The process over time is analyzed in Gorga (1991a), an unpublished paper which, as a referee of the *Journal of Economic Theory* recognized, contains a "new analytic engine" (*Anon.* 1991). Over time, the growth of values of production, distribution, and consumption leaves behind traces of motion that are an indication of their inner dynamics. Monetary wealth (MW) can be expected to soon leave the initial condition of equilibrium (0, 0, 0) and, spurred by the relative facility with which monetary instruments can be produced, grows at a faster rate than the trajectory of real wealth (RW). Also, since the pattern of distribution of ownership rights over real and monetary wealth is known to remain rather static over time; their trajectories can be represented by a straight line identified as DO. Over time, eliminating all (short and long term, cyclical, random, or aperiodic) loops, breaks, and turns, the system as a whole can be expected to leave behind idealized trajectories as in this figure:

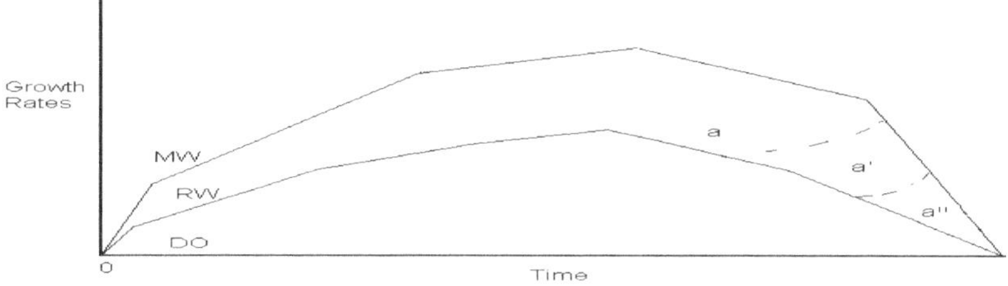

Figure 6. Trajectories of the System as a Whole.

The separation of monetary from real values becomes evident in this figure, which finally gives the definition of the "bubble". Substituting equations and real numbers for the lines of each figure reproduced above, this framework of analysis will acquire predictive value. For instance, area "a"—with its alternative sub-areas a' and a"—attempts to describe the condition of disequilibrium that gradually develops between monetary and real wealth and suggests that the smaller this area, the smaller the loss of real income over time. How to close the gap between the real and the monetary economy in the shortest possible time is clearly a problem of control, namely, a problem of economic policy—the problem of creating a just and sustainable economy.

Ever since economics was intellectually separated from morality, economic policy has become so rudderless as to lose any sense of direction. The formulation of economic policy has been abandoned to the various schools of economic thought, which, in the presence of the ongoing crisis in economic theory, are unavoidably guided, in ascending order, by petty party politics, ideology, and philosophy. And the practice of economic policy has been abandoned to bankers (as far as monetary policy is concerned) and politicians (as far as fiscal policy is concerned). Definitely there is no integrated policy concerning the stewardship of our natural resources; no integrated industrial policy; no integrated labor policy. The discovery of the economics of Moses and Jesus leaves not one scintilla of doubt: For economic policy to recover its sense of direction, it has to fill the chasm between what is and what ought to be.

The transmission belt that for millennia has carried economic theory into economic policy is the theory of economic justice. This is a theory that, while remaining astonishingly constant as a framework of analysis from Aristotle to the Doctors of the Church, allowed for continuous adaptations to the circumstances of the moment. It was divided into two planks: distributive and commutative justice. Distributive justice guided rules and regulations that govern the division of wealth once it is created; commutative justice guided rules and regulations that govern the transferal of wealth between buyers and sellers at the moment of the exchange. While the Doctors of the Church left much room for discretion in the determination of distributive justice to the parties involved in the economic process, they reached a very specific conclusion as to the dictates of commutative justice: The commutation of wealth, namely the exchange of wealth occurs in accordance with principles of justice only if it occurs on the basis of a free market price—a price determined in a market not dominated by monopolistic forces.

This robust theory was silently decapitated with the separation of economics from morality fully operated by Adam Smith—and, in part, by some of his precursors and nearly all his followers (see Fanfani, 2003, esp. p. 121). The theory of economic justice has disappeared from our consciousness; what we hear is only a faint echo of its splendor in the vague aspirations of the doctrines of "social justice". Truth to tell, the act of decapitation was facilitated by the fact that the theory of economic justice was never presented with a visible head. People with direct or, through the commons (for millennia the safety valve to preserve the dignity of the poor), indirect access to land and natural resources participated in the economic process as a matter of fact and as a consequence of an unspoken set of rights. Hence, it never occurred to Aristotle or the Doctors of the Church to make explicit the requirements of a third plank that might be called participative justice (Gorga 1999). For a great variety of reasons, those conditions are no longer in existence. Today, one has to beg in order to participate in the economic process. And if one does not take part in it, one is marginalized; one is shunted to the margins of society. Hence the plank of participative justice must be added explicitly to the theory of economic justice. Once that is done, one is presented with a framework of analysis that can be represented as follows:

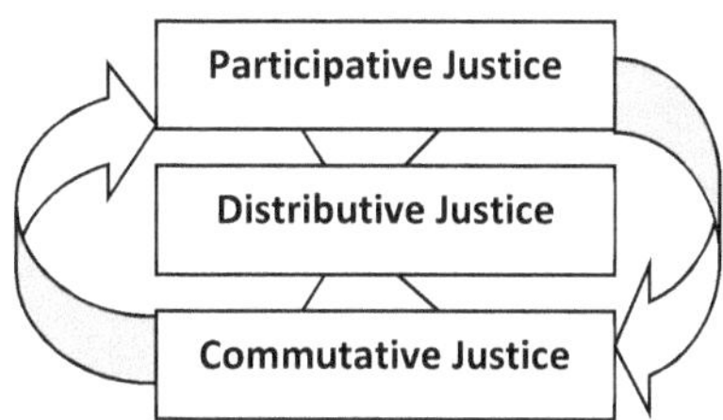

Figure 7. Economic Justice

As it can be seen, figure 7 is a mirror image of figure 6. Since the distribution of ownership rights is an inherent part of the economic process, economic justice is a natural extension of economics. One can just as soon separate the economic process from the theory of economic justice as one can separate a person from his shadow. Given this condition, a minimum set of questions to be asked in the evaluation of any economic policy are the following ones: Does the proposed policy favor participation in the creation of wealth? Does it allow for a fair distribution of the wealth thus created? Does it allow for a fair transfer of wealth from one person to another? This is the way we are going to insert the principles informing the economics of Moses and the economics of Jesus into the economic structure of the modern world.

Staying away from broad and elaborate discussions does not necessarily imply the wisdom of staying away from the specifics of the case. The specific question is: How can we transfer the principles of economic justice into the complexities of the modern economy?

Updating Economic Practice

The transmission belt that carries the theory of economic justice into practice, and shapes objective guidelines for the formulation and evaluation of just economic policies, is the reality of economic rights and economic responsibilities. They come forward as responses to the well-known requirements of the factors of production identified by Classical economists as land, capital, and labor—with the addition of a distinction between financial capital and physical capital. Our focus of attention is on the plank of participative justice; successive iterations that are mostly skipped in this presentation would reveal that the same economic rights and responsibilities satisfy also the requirements of the planks of distributive and commutative justice. A minimal set of economic rights and corresponding responsibilities is as follows.

1. *We all have the right of access to land and natural resources.* This is a natural right. It belongs to us just in virtue of our humanness. Land and natural resources are our original commons. They belong to all. This is an essential right, because without the possibility of exercising it, we are deprived of the possibility of participating in the economic process. And without this participation, we are marginalized; we are made dependent on the good will of others. The most direct way of securing this right in the complexity of the modern world is through the exercise of **the responsibility to pay taxes** for the exclusive use of those resources that are under our command (cf. Kelly 2004))—with a corresponding reduction of taxes on buildings and man-made improvements on the land. Land that sits idle does not produce income, yet it produces capital appreciation over time. Land taxation is the economic bridge between hoarding, namely the accumulation of idle land, and the right of access to that land with its natural resources. Paying taxes on the value of land and natural resources gradually encourages dis-hoarding, hence it lowers the price of the land, and correspondingly opens up the resources of that land to all those who need them and can make use of them. Worrisome hoarding is especially that which occurs both downtown and in the belt surrounding major cities and towns: it is to leapfrog over this belt that people go to the suburbs in search for affordable land, thus creating overstretched lines of communication and protection and overlong commuting lines—with consequent waste of fuel that overtaxes nonrenewable resources, the ozone layer, and the pocketbook. Paying taxes on land values is a most fair form of taxation, because it implies returning to the community part of the value that is created, not by the individual owner, but by the community. And still there is no compulsion in this policy: pay more taxes and keep control over

more land. In fact, it can even be said that this mechanism is an equivalent of the original Jubilee concerning land. (To see how this pair meets also the requirements of distributive and commutative justice, let us simply consider that, if one avoids taxes, the total tax load is not going to be distributed fairly among the population. And if one avoids taxes, one obtains something—i.e., private control over a quantity of resources—for which he does not offer proportionate compensation to the rest of the community.)

When fully explored in its dynamic elements, it will be seen that the eventual implementation of this first set of economic rights and responsibilities leads to the creation of a just and sustainable national economic policy concerning the utilization of land and natural resources.

2. *We all have the right of access to national credit.* Since national credit is the power of a nation to create money, and since the value of money is given by the value of wealth left over by past generations and the creativity of every person in a nation, national credit is the last frontier, the last commons. Without access to credit today one is made economically impotent. Worse, since this advantage is automatically granted to the privileged few, it is automatically denied to the majority of the population who are henceforth condemned to pay a higher rate of interest, if they obtain credit at all. Of course, such a loan should be extended only on the basis of **the responsibility to repay the loan**. And these loans will have a high chance of being repaid because they ought to be issued at cost and issued exclusively to individually owned and operated enterprises, Employee Stock Ownership Plans (ESOPs), and cooperatives (and states and municipalities) and issued exclusively for capital formation, namely for the creation of new wealth— not to buy financial paper, consumer goods or goods to be hoarded. Capital credit liberates people, while consumer credit enslaves them.

When fully explored in its dynamic elements, it will be seen that the eventual implementation of this second set of economic rights and responsibilities leads to the creation of a just and sustainable national economic policy concerning the utilization of our financial resources.

3. *We all have the right to the fruits of our labor.* This right should not be limited to the right to obtain only a wage. It should be extended to cover the other major fruit of economic growth over time: capital appreciation—as well as being subject to

capital loss, of course. The only justification for reserving the right to capital appreciation to stockholders, the owners of a corporation, and excluding workers from it, can be found in the fact that loans are given only to owners of past wealth (the Catch-22 of today's economic reasoning: "save and invest and you too can become rich"—as if this were either economically feasible or an ecologically sustainable proposition). But from now on this right can be extended to people who do not have prior wealth through the right of access to national credit—especially by legally transforming workers into owners through individually owned enterprises, Employee Stock Ownership Plans (ESOPs), and cooperatives. Of course, this full right should be extended only in correspondence with **the responsibility to offer services** of value equivalent to projected compensation. And there will be an outpouring of such services because, while in a command and control economy workers are requested to check their brain at the factory gate, in a moral economy workers/owners are legally and psychologically empowered to exercise their brain fully at their work post. Indeed, by linking costs of production with individual producers, current incentives to overextend business enterprises and to overexploit land, natural, and financial resources will be abated.

When fully explored in its dynamic elements, it will be seen that the eventual implementation of this third set of economic rights and responsibilities leads to the creation of a just and sustainable national economic policy concerning the utilization of our labor resources.

4. *We all have the right to protect our wealth.* This right seems to be universally accepted, except in one case that matters most: in the case of the trustification process, the process used especially after the Civil War in the United States to create corporate trusts and repeated in a hundred subtle variations ever since all over the world. (People felt free, not only to acquire shares of the stock of one corporation, but free to use that stock to acquire another whole corporation by all forms of trusts, mergers, and acquisition. The very idea of the corporation, forever a public entity, was then privatized and monetized.) There are two ways in which most corporations grow: One is through internal growth, and this approach ought to be protected in no uncertain terms; the other is growth by external purchase, and this manifestation ought to be prohibited in no uncertain terms. Why? Because this prohibition is the only certain way to protect the wealth of present owners. And if it is assumed that most stockholders of the modern corporation are happy to have their shares bought and sold on the market, it must be granted that growth-by-purchase takes wealth away from workers who have contributed to create that value—and many times, in the trustification process, lose their work site as well. All in the name of efficiency—

a misnomer that stands for private financial gain generated at the expense of shifting costs onto the community. Of course, this right ought to be purchased only at the cost of **the responsibility to respect the wealth of others**. These are two way streets. We cannot even attempt to restrain the Pac-Man economy, while we use Pac-Man instruments.

When fully explored in its dynamic elements, it will be seen that the eventual implementation of this fourth set of economic rights and responsibilities leads to the creation of a just and sustainable national economic policy concerning the utilization of our physical capital resources.

Somewhat more detailed analyses of these economic rights and responsibilities are contained in Gorga (1959, 1964, 1987, 1988, 1991b, 1994, 1997, 1999, and 2002). These economic rights and responsibilities can be applied by everyone who does not only want to receive economic justice, but also wants to grant economic justice to everyone else. Operating as tipping points (Gladwell 2000) in our reasoning and *modus vivendi*, they will allow us to extend economic freedom to all. A process of mutual interdependence will be set in place to respect not only the reality of economic affairs, but especially the reality of human relationships. Income and wealth will be distributed fairly. There will not be any need for redistribution programs; as an added bonus, lacking fuel at both ends, violent oscillations in the business cycle will be abated.

We will then recover the essential truth of the economics of Moses and the economics of Jesus. This is the truth that that there are two essential conditions of growth: economic freedom and economic justice (as concrete expressions of freedom and morality). The relationship between them is quite clear: While freedom does not necessarily bring justice with it, justice unavoidably brings freedom. One can abuse freedom, one can never abuse justice. Hence, the initial condition of freedom is proof positive of the existence of economic justice in the land.

Conclusion

The economics of Jesus is a restatement of the economics of Moses that can be applied right now, because, in the end, economics is not a dismal science, or the science of making the rich richer. It is a moral science. And, as a science, it can be applied everywhere; it can be applied by everyone—allowing us to tend our vineyard in sheer jubilation for being alive.

By casting away the economics of avarice, envy, and grumbling, if we consistently apply just economic policies for at least ten years we will discover that abject poverty disappears from the face of the earth and the rich grow steadily richer, all the while the despoliation of the land is abated. The reason for this prediction is clear. With economic freedom at large in the land, people will start producing all the wealth that they need. (Indeed, they will start creating only the children they can possibly love.) And since they will directly bear the costs associated with such production, they will produce just what they need—and not one whiff more. The avoidance of inefficiency and waste will be the lodestar to guide production as well as consumption of wealth. Mother earth with her flowers and trees and beasts will be rediscovered as the gentle giver of life and will again be considered as sacred—sacred, just as men and women are sacred; just as the whole universe is sacred.

One disclaimer concerning originality is due at this point. Having labored in the vineyard delimited by the proposition that investment is income minus hoarding for about forty years and discovering, not just while writing this paper, but only while writing the appropriate paragraph in this paper that, rather than being an original proposition, that was the fundamental proposition of the Parable of the Talents, this writer is perhaps beginning to learn how to listen (Ps 95:7-11), and these final considerations are a first result of this listening. Just as the economics of Moses and the economics of Jesus belong to Moses and to Jesus, so their translation into economic theory belongs to Keynes on the one hand and the probing questioning of Franco Modigliani on the other; and their translation into economic policy belongs to Benjamin Franklin, Henry George, Louis D. Brandeis, and Louis O. Kelso. To be noticed is that this economic policy is an all-American affair.

Appendix A

On the Modern Attempt at Separating Economics from Morality

From Moses to Adam Smith everyone agreed that economic activity occurs within the context of the moral law—thus continuing without a hiatus the tradition of the Jewish Law. Enter Adam Smith, a professor, not of economics, but of moral philosophy and—at first following and then leading, a whole set of well-known complex historical and cultural events—economics becomes separated from morality. No matter what he said in his *Theory of Moral Sentiments*, a work that very few have ever read, in the *Wealth of Nations*, the foundation stone of modern economics, Adam Smith makes no reference to economic justice and five references to morality, all offensively disparaging. No wonder he was unable to fulfill his promise to write a treatise that would potentially unify all social sciences (1759, last par.; 1790, A2). Gradually the importance of morality in economics does not only go unrecognized; it is firmly denied. This breach in such a long tradition has been bored into our minds through this doubt: Does not morality lead to inefficiency? So deep is this bore that, in the name of economic efficiency, namely a presumed inefficiency of morality (please notice the unspoken subtle change of words), the Immoral Economy is tolerated at nearly every level of the discussion. Just as Jesus cast away the money changers from the Temple of his day, so he would certainly cast away the word changers from the temple of thought of today. The Immoral Economy is not tenable—neither from an economic point of view nor from an intellectual point of view.

The Immoral Economy Is Not Tenable from an Economic Point of View

The assumption of a presumed inefficiency of morality is so central to modern thinking yet so contrary to the composition of reality that one marvels how it can receive such widespread submissive assent. The assumption is based, not on sound macroeconomic reasoning and comprehensive accounting, but on a series of blatant shortcuts. At the very core of economic theory there is a transposition of the tool of measurement with the object of measurement. The tool of measurement is money; the object of measurement is economic activity. Because of the transposition of these two elements, everything in mainstream economics is reduced to money—and human beings, if they enter the equations at all, are reduced to rational automatons.

59

The most immediate effect of this shortcut is that the monetary economy obliterates the vision of the real economy: in mainstream economics there is no accounting of stocks of natural resources or stocks of real goods and services. No wonder Wall Street analysts reduce the whole of economics to the "bottom line" and everyone is expected to give assent to their valuation. Please note that the vaunted economic efficiency is thus reduced to monetary efficiency. The consequences of this reduction, just as the consequences of the reduction of biology to sex, are shunted aside by a shortsighted understanding and a deficient measurement of efficiency: first, the efficiency of the Gross National Product is always measured in the short run, whereby the cost of depressions and recessions is not taken into account; second, the measurement of the efficiency of the Gross National Product does not take into account the Gross National Cost represented by overexploitation of the land and of human beings, who are treated like commodities/machines requested to work harder and harder, faster and faster—or are cast aside onto the sidewalks of our cities and towns; third, the efficiency of the firm does not take into account the cost of externalities, an economic category that insulates the firm from the rest of society: the more such costs (costs of pollution, costs of pension plans, medical costs) are calculated as external to the firm, the better it is for the bottom line of course; and, finally, the cost of labor does not take into account the cost of welfare programs, most of which issue an essential subsidy to underpaid workers. No wonder monetary efficiency is exalted and economic morality is berated: private interests enjoy all the profits; the general public bears all the costs. Fools are treated like fools. In the reality of economics—the morality of economics—costs can be shifted onto other shoulders, but they do not go away. The unity of economics and morality is a matter internal to the economic system; it can be hidden but it cannot be destroyed. The Immoral Economy is not an economic necessity determined by "efficiency"—quite the contrary. Clearly, the Immoral Economy is not the result of "blind forces"; it is not the result of an "invisible hand". The Immoral Economy is the result of immoral choices by the hands of very visible human beings.

The Immoral Economy Is Not Tenable from an Intellectual Point of View

The battering ram used to transform the small, no matter how unfounded, doubt about the inefficiency of morality into the rout of morality has been a peculiar understanding of freedom. Insulated from the rest of the universe, this word has been insulated from rational analysis. Would I release to you control over my freedom? Certainly not! The beginning of wisdom lies in the realization that neither words nor even sentences stand alone. Do two parallel lines meet?

The modern understanding of freedom, in fact, is propped up with a web of intellectual relationships that has gradually yielded the construction of a full-fledged system of thought known as modern rationalism. When individual propositions are analyzed as part of this system of thought, they do not stand to reason. In this system of thought, morality is reduced to a null set because the meaning of freedom has become so tenuous, so empty of content as to be elevated to the rank of infinity; the idea of freedom has been raised to such altitudes as to become an absolute value. This elevation is made plausible because the entire intellectual system of rationalism, just like modern economic analysis that stands at its core, is ahistorical. If observed in the reality of history, it becomes incontrovertible that freedom in general and economic freedom in particular is not absolute. First of all, unbridled economic freedom is a good that is restricted for the consumption of the few; indeed, unbridled economic freedom for the few is acquired at the cost of subjection for the many. If it were an absolute value, unbridled freedom would be able to be extended to all. Those who disagree with this statement are compelled to admit to the existence of different degrees of freedom. Yet, again, if it were an absolute value, unbridled freedom would be able to be extended to all in identical parts. By the same token, if it were an absolute value, unbridled freedom's life would be extended forever.

The historic evidence to the contrary is provided by economic dynamics—more than any other discipline. The evidence is so rich one marvels how the elevation of freedom to such height can receive so little examination and so widespread submissive assent. Freedom is not enough for sustainable growth. On the contrary, the repeated history of business enterprise upon business enterprise and indeed the apparent history of entire civilizations show that unbridled freedom inevitably leads to libertinism, which gradually destroys freedom and then civilization itself.

The destruction of enterprises and the destruction of civilizations might take some time. There are other effects that are immediate. The elevation of freedom to the status of an absolute carries with it the destruction, not so much of religion—which is wanted and expected—as the destruction of the sense of community. Isolated rational automatons (more commonly called economic agents, individuals, and disembodied minds), which stand at the basis of modern rationalism and especially at the basis of modern economic theory, clearly have no sense of community. It is only this lack of sense of community that ultimately explains the use of such blatant shortcuts to measure efficiency as the ones mentioned above. Automatons have no sense of responsibility toward the community. Indeed, they have no feelings; no sentiments. And as such they ultimately destroy the dignity of the human race at its deepest core.

Economics Cannot Be Separated from Morality

True efficiency is the result of morality. Economics cannot be separated from morality. Let us immediately rephrase that. Economics cannot be separated from morality without creating negative economic consequences that generally vary in accordance with the seriousness of the moral transgression. As human beings we are free, because we are called to choose—not between Gucci and Pucci—but between good and evil.

Morality is the set of rules that train the will to desire and to achieve what is positive for oneself and for others, by reconciling within oneself the forces of both freedom and authority. An undisciplined will suggests that if I steal I clearly add to my wealth. That would appear to be a positive result for me, even though negative for you. Ancient moral rules suggest that to steal is an immoral act, hence to be shunned, because it is not good for one's dignity.

Human dignity is not an abstraction. Not to have dignity means not to be fully human. Not to be fully human means to be either like beasts, thereby having no creativity and no freedom, or like stones thereby having no feelings of pain or joy in addition to no freedom.

Appendix B

Hoarding for Doubters

This writer has spent many years in the vineyard delimited by the proposition that Investment is Income minus Hoarding. And still he tends to lose sight of the fact that, for many complex reasons, most economists do not—and cannot—see hoarding. They do not physically see hoarding; hence, they intellectually deny its existence. The issue is not one of economics. The issue is one of mathematics and logic: once the economic reality is described by the given definitions of saving and consumption, saving becomes "equal" to investment (cf. Keynes 1936, p. 63), and no space is left for hoarding. It is to be noted that, as demonstrated in the text, hoarding was well known and widely discussed from Jesus to Locke.

Due to the new framework of analysis designed by this writer (Gorga 2002, pp. 23-40, 67-158, 303-328), it is again possible to speak of hoarding within the context of formal economic theory. Many consequences ensue from the existence of hoarding (cf. *ibid.,* pp. 235-302, 329-358). Yet, even accepting the validity of the new intellectual construction that includes hoarding in its purview, a doubt persists about the existence of hoarding (see Broski 2003).

This doubt is creating an interesting consequence that can be explained only in terms of the relationship between intellectual paradigms and real phenomena. Thomas E. Kuhn in *The Structure of Scientific Revolutions* pointed out that the prevailing paradigm in physics for a long time made scientists see a substance, phlogiston, which eventually turned out to be a non-existent element. In economics today, there is a reverse chain of causation. Since economists deny the existence of hoarding, they tend to conclude that there is no reason for a new intellectual construction such as elaborated in Gorga (2002) that unarguably, again, permits its vision.

This Appendix therefore attempts to clarify three questions: What is hoarding? Is there any hoarding? Who does the hoarding? This exposition also makes it clear that hoarding has a direct effect on both the projection of future economic activity and the understanding of the General Theory.

What Is Hoarding?

Hoarding is the act of keeping wealth in an idle state. Hoarding is the act of keeping wealth in an idle state *for any reason apart from a technical requirement for keeping it idle*. More specifically, hoarded is all wealth that is not used, *at the moment of the observation*, as a consumer good or a capital good. Before starting the discussion, we shall equip ourselves with an ad hoc methodology and a minimalist economic theory that will allow us to find hoarding.

Ad Hoc Methodology on How to Find Hoarding

We shall abstract from the theoretical possibility or impossibility of the existence of hoarding. We shall be totally indifferent to either one of these two theoretical possibilities.

In other words, the primary focus of this Appendix is not on any of the causes or the effects of hoarding, nor on its relationships with the canonical constellation of the component elements of economic theory, but on hoarding in itself and by itself. Yet, nothing stands alone. Therefore, at times we shall call attention to some effects of hoarding; and, given that any economic action has effects on quantities and relative prices, we shall reason by excess. Whenever necessary and appropriate, we shall run a peculiar thought experiment (cf. Kuhn 1996, p. 88); we shall assume that the entire stock of a particular item of wealth falls under the exclusive control of only one person.

A Minimalist Theory

As an inescapable consequence of the given definition of hoarding, all wealth is posited to be divided into three parts: consumer goods, capital goods, and goods hoarded. This is a minimalist theory, but a theory nonetheless. The assumption is that any item of wealth—not simply money—can be hoarded.

What Is Hoarded

Currency. Currency hoarded is the simplest case to identify. Currency under the mattress in excess of the need for daily transactions, as well as currency kept in a safe deposit box, is money hoarded. It is money kept idle. A more complex variant of this phenomenon is money that is owned by a bank while keeping it idle in a safe deposit box. That currency is also hoarded. Let us remember that the object of our observation is the specific item of wealth, not its owner, and that here we are not primarily concerned with either the causes or the effects of hoarding.

Land. Land hoarded is simple to identify. All land that is used neither as a consumer good (e.g., for recreational purposes) nor as a capital good is land hoarded. Land that is kept idle for the esthetic pleasure of looking at it is not land hoarded but land used as any other consumer good. All land that a government keeps idle for recreational purposes is not land hoarded; yet land in an unvisited park is land hoarded. Land covered with weeds and rubbish in the downtown of a city is clearly land hoarded. All uncultivated and undeveloped (landlocked) land is also hoarded. All land kept idle in a country in which there are idle hands that would till or somehow make use of it, is land that is clearly hoarded; see, e.g. latifundia.

Gold. Gold in the course of extraction and sale in a gold mine is a capital good. Gold in a microchip plant or a jeweler's workshop is also a capital good. An interesting case is the case of a gold bracelet in a jeweler's shop: this is still a capital good. It is only when the bracelet adorns a woman's wrist that the item becomes a consumer good. And what is a gold ingot at Fort Knox if not, clearly, a good hoarded? And so is the gold ingot in the safe of a bank, whether a private person or the bank itself happens to be its owner.

Supplies. Supplies are clearly capital goods; yet, even supplies can be hoarded—as they are when they are bought and kept idle for a period of time that goes beyond technical reasons for keeping them idle. One might say that when the physical flow of supplies is changed into a stock of supplies, chances are that those supplies are hoarded. When in the 70s oil was kept in tankers waiting outside harbors, that oil was hoarded. Some of this oil was hoarded to staunch the effect of expected higher prices; some of it was hoarded in fear of future exhaustion of those supplies. The reason does not matter. It is the economic condition that matters.

A coffee cup. A coffee cup in my home is a consumer good. A coffee cup in my office is a capital good. And a coffee cup in my attic is a good hoarded—unless I use it, even just once a year, on my patio during summertime.

Consumer goods. The hardest case to identify as hoarding, at least the last case that was identified by this writer, is the case of the hoarding of consumer goods. (Unless the eyes are never peeled away from the economic reality, words become utterly misleading.) Again the case of voluntary hoarding is clear. The case of the person who buys two pairs of boots because prices are skyrocketing is clear: one pair is used as consumer goods and the other is hoarded. More subtle is the case of unanticipated hoarding. Have you ever discovered in your clothes closet a shirt with its price tag still attached after a couple of years of its purchase? The item was clearly hoarded. More deviant still is the case of "consumer goods" that have lost their utility to the owner, and are hoarded because one is too lazy to offer them to others who would put them to good use.

Any item of wealth can be hoarded. During the Great Inflation of the 70s Johnny Carson, the famous comedian, one night made a joke about the disappearance of tissue paper. The day after the shelves were bare. A shortage was created because of the unexpected demand. Indeed, much of the gasoline shortage those same years was created by the fact that many drivers would tend to keep the tank constantly filled. They were hoarding gasoline.

Stocks and bonds. Stocks and bonds are not wealth; they represent wealth. Therefore, they cannot be hoarded—even though the corporation in whose name those stocks and bonds are issued might be hoarding some real wealth on its own account. No matter how many consequences derive from accumulating even all the stock of a corporation, this action does not directly affect other people's wealth; at the limit, you can destroy all the stock certificates that you own, and you do not directly affect other people's wealth. Other people would benefit from a transfer of the title of ownership of these certificates to them, but that is a moral issue with its own indirect economic consequences. Directly, the wealth of the nation would not even minimally be affected by the destruction or transfer of stocks and bonds; indirectly, you might increase the value of the remaining stock certificates, but that would only be a monetary change. Currency is significantly different from stocks and bonds. To say the least, currency has an immediate and direct utility. Accumulate or destroy all currency, and you do not destroy the value of any real wealth; yet you immediately make all exchanges more cumbersome and gradually more expensive. As a saying once went, currency saves shoe leather. This is the cost—in real wealth—that would be incurred by the nation if all currency were destroyed.

Labor. To evaluate the full cost of hoarding incurred by a nation, one has to realize that involuntary unemployment is labor power that is hoarded. To reach an accurate measurement of this phenomenon, one has to keep in mind, first, that official unemployment rates from the ghettos to the Indian Reservations generally vary anywhere from 15% to 75%; second, that official statistics measure unemployment only among those who are still actively searching for employment: those who have given up are not counted. Another group that might be worth to look at with new eyes is the pool of officially retired people.

Is There Hoarding?

The specific question is: Is there any hoarding any time, anywhere in the world? To answer this question in relation to money, it is important to bring to mind two specific examples. First, the less developed the banking system in a country, the more hoarding takes place under the mattress. The deeper the condition of economic depression in a country, the higher the accumulation of money hoarded in a bank— by a bank. How much deeper did the Great Depression become because banks could not find borrowers for their hoards?

To clearly see hoarding, one has to make a dynamic and longitudinal analysis of the issue. One will then discover that the quantity of certain forms of hoarding increases over time. During the same period, other forms decrease: currency, for instance, is hoarded less when the prices of goods rise. (This is another variation of Gresham's

Law.) But of course the calculation has to take into account that the amount of currency in circulation depends on the will of the people as well as the willingness of the monetary system to accommodate that demand. The condition is wholly dynamic. And since in economics everything is instantaneously related to everything else, one is always faced with questions of relative values and relative prices.

These observations lead to another consideration. At first sight, one might be tempted to assume that all hoarding is "bad" or more specifically that all hoarding has negative economic effects. That is not necessarily the case. Some hoarding might cause positive effects for the individual person as well as for society as a whole. For instance, some undeveloped and uncultivated (landlocked) land might become a buried treasure for the next generation; and some money kept in a safe deposit box keeps prices rising even minimally at a slower pace. There are no general cases in economics; all cases are individual ones. That is why one cannot let "the market" make decisions for oneself.

Who Does the Hoarding?

We all hoard wealth. Some more, some less, but we all hoard wealth. Even in this brief excursus we have met governments hoarding gold, landlords hoarding land, bankers hoarding currency, industrialists hoarding supplies, and individual human beings hording consumer goods. A disclosure: This writer hoards books and computers: there are some books that he knows full well he will never get to read or no longer needs to read; there are some computers that he knows full well he will never get to use—he should give them away, instead he hoards them.

Some Concluding Comments

The existence of hoarding is proof positive of the existence of freedom, rather than determinism, in the world of economics.

As against the accumulation of goods hoarded, the consumption of consumer goods is, indeed, determined by need: needs of physical survival and needs of social status. The consumption of capital goods is also determined by the need to reduce the amount of time—or, more precisely, the amount of life—one devotes to the production of goods; the resulting free time is proof positive of the efficiency of the economic system in which one lives; to whom and to what one devotes the resulting free time is determined by the degree of civilization and spirituality stored in this person's character.

Is not the existence of hoarding, then, proof positive of the amount of freedom granted to the individual person by the economic system in which one lives? And the amount of dishoarding, by giving one's surplus wealth to the people who need it and cannot produce it for themselves, is proof positive of the degree of morality lived by the person who dishoards.

Clearly, neither consumption nor investment, but hoarding alone is wholly determined by the free will of the individual economic agent.

Hoarding is an arbitrary and subjective activity. Of course, there is much arbitrariness and subjectivity in consumption and investment as well. To say the least, then, hoarding contains a greater degree of arbitrariness and subjectivity than either consumption or investment. At the limit, as we know, differences in degree are differences in kind. Hoarding therefore is an economic activity fundamentally different from consumption and investment.

The discovery of the existence of hoarding in the economic system is not an exclusively intellectual issue. The existence of hoarding has a clear concrete effect on the measurement of economic activity. Hoarding can be measured only by working with an intimate understanding of the person who does the hoarding. All other measurements are purely arbitrary. Any projection of future economic activity that does not take the erratic nature of hoarding into full account is destined to yield only ambiguous results. More generally, any national projection of future economic activity that does not take the existence of hoarding into account is doomed to make false predictions.

It is equally worthwhile to note that the existence of hoarding has a decisive influence on the understanding of the *General Theory*. Hoarding is what fills the gap between the form and the substance of that great masterpiece. While the form is written on the basis of Keynes' model of the economic system as pointed out above, the substance of the General Theory is written in terms of the existence of hoarding. Three major pieces of evidence should suffice. First, if there were no hoarding in the economic system it would make no difference whether people had a propensity to consume a little less than one's income (Keynes 1936, p. 96), because the difference would be taken up by saving and investing. Yet, Keynes knew full well that there is hoarding in the community and therefore he specified that under given circumstances "saving and spending will *both* decrease" *(ibid.* p. 111; italics in original). With the recognition of hoarding, this observation turns out to be true in a static examination of the economic system, as well as in a dynamic investigation of the system. The second case regards Keynes' prescription for the "only radical cure for the crises of confidence which afflict the economic life of the modern world" *(ibid.* p. 161); as analyzed in Gorga (2002, esp. pp. 93-115), the prescription becomes clear only if one takes the existence of hoarding into account. Third, Keynes defined interest in an outright fashion as "the reward of not-hoarding" *(ibid.* p. 174).

Appendix C

Mathematical Models
A Progressive View of the Economic System

Eliminating all explanations concerning their derivation and the interconnections among them, this Appendix is an attempt to concentrate the mind on the basic mathematical models of the Concordian economics. These models—with key diagrams given in the text—offer a progressive view of the economic system as a whole. This process of discovery is best described by a Fields Medalist at Princeton University, William Thurston (2006, p. D1): "You don't see what you're seeing until you see it, but when you do see it, it lets you see many other things."

Flows Model
(The Revised Keynes' Model)

$$Y = C + S$$
$$I = Y - S$$
$$I = C$$

where
Y stands for Income
C for Consumption or *any* type of expenditure
S for Saving, an entity conceptually separated from Investment
I for Investment

Flows Model
with
Hoarding (H) substituted for Saving

$$Y = C + H$$
$$I = Y - H$$
$$I = C$$

$$\textbf{Flows Model}$$
$$\textbf{with}$$
$$\textbf{Production (P) substituted for Investment}$$

$$Y = C + H$$
$$P = Y - H$$
$$P = C$$

$$\textbf{Flows Model}$$
$$\textbf{With the Equality of Production and Consumption}$$
$$\textbf{Substituted with the Equivalence of Production, Distribution (D), and}$$
$$\textbf{Consumption}$$

$$Y = C + H$$
$$P = Y - H$$
$$P = D = C$$

$$\textbf{Monetary Formulation of the Flows Model}$$

$$MY = E + E_h$$

$$E_k = MY - E_h$$

$$E_k = E$$

where
MY stands for money income
E for expenditure
E_h for hoarding-expenditure, namely, money directly hoarded
and/or spent on goods hoarded
E_k for investment-expenditure

$$\textbf{Stocks Model}$$

$$\text{Wealth} = (\text{Consumer Goods} + \text{Capital Goods}) + \text{Goods Hoarded}$$
$$\text{Investment-assets} = \text{Wealth} - \text{Goods Hoarded}$$
$$\text{Investment-assets} = \text{Consumer Goods} + \text{Capital Goods}$$

Model of Production

$$P = CG + KG + GH$$

$$KG = P - (GH + CG)$$

$$KG = OKG$$

where

CG stands for Consumer Goods
KG for Capital Goods
GH for Goods Hoarded
OKG for value of Ownership of Capital Goods

Model of Distribution

D = OCG + OKG + OGH

OKG = D – (OGH + OCG)

OKG = I

where

D stands for Distribution or Real Income observed from the point of view of distribution of ownership rights
OCG for value of Ownership of Consumer Goods
OKG for value of Ownership of Capital Goods
OGH for value of Ownership of Goods Hoarded

Model of Consumption

$$C = E_h + E$$

$$I = C - E_h$$

$$I = E$$

where

C stands for Consumption or Money Income observed

from the point of view of consumption

E_h for money reserved for Hoarding-Expenditure

E for money reserved for Expenditure (on consumer goods and capital goods)

I for Investment

**Synthetic Model of the Economic System as a Whole
(From Gorga 1991a)**

$$p^{\cdot} = fp(p,d,c)$$
$$d^{\cdot} = fd(p,d,c)$$
$$c^{\cdot} = fc(p,d,c)$$

where

$p^{\cdot}$ stands for rate of change in total production

d for rate of change in the values of distribution of ownership rights

$c^{\cdot}$ for rate of change in total expenditure.

References

Allen, R. G. D. 1970. *Mathematical Economic,* 2nd ed., London and New York: Macmillan, St. Martin's.

Anon. 1991. "Referee Report, 'The Dynamics of the Economic System,' by Carmine Gorga." *J Econ. Theory*, # 91297.

Brady, Michael Emmett. 2004a. *Essays on J. M. Keynes and...* Xlibris Corporation.

_____. 2004b. *J. M. Keynes' Theory of Decision Making, Induction, and Analogy.* Xlibris Corporation.

_____. 2006. *The Applied Mathematics of J.M. Keynes' Theory of Effective Demand in the General Theory.* Xlibris Corporation.

Broski, Mark. 2003. "The Economic Process: An Instantaneous Non-Newtonian Picture. Carmine Gorga." *Journal of Markets and Morality* 6, no. 1: 297-98.

Catherine of Siena. 1980. *The Dialogue.* S. Noffke trans. Mahwah NJ: The Paulist Press.

Chapra, Umer M. 1985. *Towards a Just Monetary System.* Leicester, UK: The Islamic Foundation.

Fanfani, Amintore. 2003. Catholicism, Protestantism, and Capitalism. Norfolk, VA: IHS Press.

Foley, Duncan K. 2006. *Adam's Fallacy: A Guide to Economic Theology*. Cambridge, MA/ London, UK: Belknap Press of Harvard University Press.

Gladwell, Malcolm. 2000. *The Tipping Point: How Little Things Can Make a Big Difference*. NY: Little, Brown & Company.

Goldsmith, Raymond W. 1955-1956. *A Study of Saving in the United States*, 3 Vols. Princeton: Princeton University Press.

Gorga, Carmine. 1959. *A Synthesis of the Political Thought of Louis D. Brandeis*. Graduation Dissertation University of Naples.

_____. 1964. "Not Simply a National Fund, but a Stabilization and Development Fund", *Mondo Economico*, 19 (14) 14-16.

_____. 1982. "The Revised Keynes' Model" (an Abstract), Atlantic Econ. J. 10:3, p. 52.

_____and Norman G. Kurland. 1987. "The Productivity Standard: A True Golden Standard," in *Every Worker An Owner: A Revolutionary Free Enterprise Challenge to Marxism,* D. M. Kurland, ed. Washington, DC: Center for Economic and Social Justice.

_____ and Louis J. Ronsivalli. 1988. *Quality Assurance of Seafood*. New York: Van Nostrand Reinhold.

_____. 1991a. "The Dynamics of the Economic System," unpub. man.

_____. 1991b. "Bold New Directions in Politics and Economics," *The Human Economy Newsletter,* 12:1, pp. 3-6, 12.

______ . 1994. "Four Economic Rights: Social Renewal Through Economic Justice for All," *Social Justice Rev.* 85:1-2, pp. 3-6.

______ and Stuart B. Weeks. 1997. "Fisheries Renewal: A Renewal of the Soul of Business," *Catholic Social Science Rev.* 2, pp. 145-161.

______ . 1998. "The Creators of Poverty," *Gloucester Daily Times,* **Symposium**, December 18, p. A10.

______ . 1999. "Toward the Definition of Economic Rights," *J. Markets and Morality,* 2:1, pp. 88-101.

______ . 2002. *The Economic Process: An Instantaneous Non-Newtonian Picture.* Lanham, MD and Oxford: University Press of America.

Harris, Maria. 1996. *Proclaim Jubilee! A Spirituality for the Twenty-First Century.* Louisville, KY: Westminster John Knox Press.

Hayek, Friedrick A. 1963. "The Economics of the 1930s as Seen from London," in *Contra Keynes and Cambridge: Essays and Correspondence* (vol. 9 of *The Collected Works of F. A. Hayek*), Bruce Caldwell, ed. 49. Chicago: University of Chicago Press (1995).

______. 1994. *Hayek on Hayek: An Autobiographical Dialogue.* Stephen Kresge and Leif Wenar, eds. Chicago: University of Chicago Press. Quoted in Bruce Caldwell, *Hayek's Challenge: An Intellectual Biography of F. A. Hayek.* Chicago: University of Chicago Press, 2004, p. 401.

Kelly, John L. 2004. "The Tithe: Land Rent to God," *Acton Institute Religion & Liberty,* July and August.

Keynes, J. Maynard. 1936. *The General Theory of Employment, Interest, and Money*. NY: Harcourt.

_____. 1973. *The Collected Writings of John Maynard Keynes*, D. E. Moggridge, ed., Vol. XIV (London, New York and Toronto: Macmillan, St. Martin's Press.

Kuhn, Thomas S. 1996 ed. *The Structure of Scientific Revolutions*. Chicago and London: University of Chicago Press.

Locke, John. 1698. *Two Treatises of Government*. London: Awnsham and John Churchill. Laslett P. ed. NY: A Mentor Book (1965).

Modigliani, Franco. 1980. *The Collected Papers of Franco Modigliani. Vol. 1: Essays in Macroeconomics*. Abel, A. ed. Cambridge MA and London, UK: MIT Press.

Samuelson, Paul A. 1946. "The General Theory," in *Keynes' General Theory: Reports of Three Decades*, R. Lekachman, ed. (New York and London: St. Martin's, Macmillan Press, 1964).

Schumpeter, Joseph A. 1936. "The general theory of employment, interest and money," *J. Amer. Statistical Assoc.* 31, pp. 791-95.

Smith, Adam. 1759. *The Theory of Moral Sentiments*. London: A. Millar, 1790. Sixth edition.

_____. 1776. *An Inquiry into the Nature and Causes of the Wealth of Nations*. London: Methuen and Co., Ltd., ed. Edwin Cannan, 1904. Fifth edition.

Tierney, Brian. 1959. *Medieval Poor Law: A Sketch of Canonical Theory and Its Application in England*. Berkeley: University of California Press.

Thompson, J. M. T. 1986. *Nonlinear Dynamics and Chaos, Geometric Methods for Engineers and Scientists*. New York: Wiley.

Thurston, William. 2006. Quoted in Dennis Overbye, "An Elusive Proof and Its Elusive Prover: That rabbit is actually a sphere. (Read on.) But the man who proved it is missing," *New York Times*, August 15.

Trocmé, André. 1973. *Jesus and the Nonviolent Revolution.* Scottdale PA, Kitchener: Ont.: Herald Press.

Wood, Diane. 2002. *Medieval Economic Thought*. Cambridge, UK: Cambridge University Press.

Zona, Guy A. 1994. *The Soul Would Have No Rainbow if the Eyes had no Tears – and Other Native American Proverbs*. N.Y: Simon and Schuster.

Chapter 3: Cancel Student Debt?
NO!! Cancel ALL Debt

We hear much of cancellation of student debt. While a worthy effort, not much thought has been given to its implications. And I do not mean economic implications alone. Let us start with a brief examination of a few social implications.

Social Implications

When you give special treatment to any segment of society, you inevitably segment society into pieces - and you automatically sow seeds of destruction. You set one group against another.

No. You should not do that. Are not people whose mortgages are "underwater" deserving of such equitable treatment as cancellation of their debts? One can argue that they are *more* deserving because, while students *knew* they were incurring debt with the accumulation of interest, and compound interest, mortgage holders did not know that "the Market" would cause a collapse of the value of their houses.

"Are you saying that some are "first-class" citizens? Who is to judge?"

No. You cannot be the judge of who is "more" deserving than the other.

Worse. Are you saying that some are "first-class" citizens? Who is to judge?

Political Implications

When you set one group against the other or even more simply temporarily you set one *before* the other, you are destined to fail politically. To win such awesome social and political battles as cancellation of debts on a systematic basis, you need the broadest possible coalition of citizens. To select one group for "preferential treatment" is politically self-defeating.

Theological Implications

Moses and Jesus, as they so evidently did, *invoked* powers of a higher order when they advocated the cancellation of debts. [Yes, Virginia. The Israelites had the wisdom to implement Moses' recommendations, and so did many Kings and Emperors over the years upon installation.] As Transcendentalists, New Agers, and Mystics of all ages and traditions have always known, we have to be in the *same spirit* to win. The program of cancellation of debts has to be our common goal; it has to be a systematic program.

Above all, it has to be designed to benefit the entire population.

Financial Implications

Paolo Uccello, a Florentine painter of the Quattrocento, seems to have been so in love with the newly discovered prospective that he would abandon his conjugal bed in favor of practicing with and proclaiming the beauty of the new tools. Unfortunately, there is no similar anecdote to diffuse the importance of double-entry bookkeeping, an invention by Luca Pacioli, a Tuscan Franciscan, at about the same time. But the science of finance has had, and might still have, deeper implications for humanity than the exploration of the perspective.

"there is no such thing as an externality."

The Beauty, Truth, and Goodness of Double-Entry Bookkeeping. Double-Entry Bookkeeping is a construction of beauty. This is a self-evident characteristic. What is not generally emphasized is that this technique allows us to discover *the truth* about personal, corporate, and governmental affairs. As such it has done and can do *much good* for mankind. But, like any tool, just as it has the potential for good it can also be used to commit much mischief. The biggest mischiefs are those allowed by economists with their fictitious construction of externalities. Mother

Earth suffers most from this lie: If you look at the world as a whole, you discover that there is no such thing as an externality.

Recently, very recently, I made a discovery that might set straight a few millennia of abuse of the lender: The lender, I discovered, is <u>not a hoarder</u>. And then the function of interest, as Keynes intuited, interest as counted in accounting books, became utterly clear: Interest is the reward of not hoarding.

Would the world be better off if people with extra money in their pockets were to hoard their financial assets?

This is a question too deep to explore in these lines. It is the reverse perspective that is of interest at the moment. Much bookkeeping is built on the addition and subtraction of zeros. If you add them - or subtract them - systematically, you do not affect human, substantive relationships one iota. People are just as "rich" as they were before.

If we build on this simple verity, we might avert the impending disaster that is ready to engulf us in a sea of indebtedness. Zeros have been compounded so fast and furiously that we cannot grasp them any longer. If we grasp them by the tail, and <u>systematically reduce them</u> on a recurring cycle every seven years, as Moses advocated and the Israelites were wise enough to put into action, we will all be that much richer together.

If not, we will likely plunge into an abyss with no light in sight.

How Can We See the Light?

Just as recently as the last few days, I believe I have seen a ray of light out of the current morass. With a new twinkle in my eye, I have lately suggested that the Federal Reserve System, and all other Central Banks of the world, can set - anew - our financial fortunes on a steady and just path if they create a <u>new monetary unit for us</u>. Offering a nod of approval to Keynes, I have suggested that our Central Banks ought to create the American Bancor, the Swiss Bancor, the Russian Bancor, the Chinese Bancor.

"Much bookkeeping is built on the addition and subtraction of zeros."

The prerequisite is that the new currency be issued following three rules recommended by <u>Concordian monetary policy</u>. New money should be created <u>as a loan</u>:

1. only to create real wealth of tables and chairs, not to purchase financial instruments;
2. to individual entrepreneurs, cooperatives, corporations with ESOPs and/or CSOPs in their constitutions, and public agencies with taxing power so that the loan can be repaid;
3. at cost.

We thus divert national credit from Wall Street to Main Street.

Toward a World Without Reserve Currencies

If the new money is created on the basis of identical rules all over the world, there will <u>not be any need for reserve currencies</u>. With the help of today's computers, we will know the respective value of each currency at each instant in time. A fundamental condition for mutual respect will thus be established among the nations.

Trade wars? Why trade wars any longer?

Toward a World Without Fear of Crashes

If the flow of new money is directed toward Main Street, let the crash of the financial system come. The sooner the better. No damage will be done to the real economy.

The behemoths of international finance will collapse. They periodically collapse because their design is structurally unsound: Infinite debt does not exist. They should no longer be artificially revived with the taxpayer and bank depositors' money.

'The systematic, periodic cancellation of debts is going to create economic freedom for all on earth"

Few jobs will be lost - at no damage to anyone. Those who want to enjoy retirement, they can; they have accumulated the means to live comfortably. Those who want to start the business of their dreams, they have the knowledge to do so: provided they will create new real wealth, the "new" money will be available to them as well as to any other entrepreneur. Those who might want to remain in the banking business, they only need to inform local banks of their availability.

Economic Implications

What are the economic implications of winning the struggle *for* the <u>systematic, continuous</u> cancellation of debts, as Moses advocated and Jesus in the *Our Father* singled out? The result is going to be as revolutionary as anyone has ever dared to dream. The systematic, periodic cancellation of debts is going to create economic freedom for all on earth; the creation and distribution of money along sacred principles of justice will allow us to create all the real wealth that we individually need.

We shall then no longer be blind followers of the "dismal science"; rather, we will be happily practicing <u>The Economics of Jubilation</u>.

If we adopt these two measures in the immediate future : Strengthen the social safety net and cancel all debt, we will all do well.

Next order of business is to redirect national credit from Wall Street to Main Street. But that can wait for the next communication titled *From the 'Dismal Science' to The Economics of Jubilation through Concordian economics.*

If we do redirect national credit from Wall Street to Main Street, businesses will recover and a powerful program of investment in social and physical infrastructure will become possible. To suffer from shortage of money in the Digital Age is foolhardy; if we waste not, we will want not. Doing things for others as well as for ourselves, we will survive with greater social cohesion than we have lately had. We will become individually and socially stronger.

How can we survive the transition from here to there? To keep us united and aware of our progress, we can study and sign these two Internet petitions:

✓ MEND THE FED   http://petitions.moveon.org/sign/a-patriotic-petition-1?source=c.em&r_by=2016207
✓ DEFUSE THE BOMB http://petitions.moveon.org/sign/the-jubilee-solution, the bomb of a financial crash at any stage in its development.

***

Our legislators are mostly accustomed to listening to lobbyists. Lobbyists necessarily speak for private interests. We must speak for the common good—and we will be listened to.

About the Author

Carmine Gorga, a former Fulbright Scholar, is president of The Somist Institute. He is the founder of Concordian economics. He has published eight books and numerous papers, many in peer-reviewed journals. Dr. Gorga is a regular contributor to *Mother Pelican, OpEdNews, TalkMarkets,* and *Econintersect.*

Econintersect is among the Top 100 Sites for Enlightened Economists.

His fundamental book, titled The Economic Process: An Instantaneous Non-Newtonian Picture, has been annotated twice in *Journal of Economic Literature* (JEL). In its -- second -- annotation, December 2017 issue (p. 1642), JEL states: "Expanded third edition presents the transformation of economic theory into Concordian economics, shifting the understanding of the economic system from a mechanical, Newtonian entity to a more dynamic, relational process."

Fifty years in the making, Concordian economics is a new/old paradigm that, in the words of Vincent Ferrini, "has the answers to universal poverty and the anxieties of the affluent."

Reviewing his latest paper titled "Concordian economics - An Integration of Theory, Policy, and Practice," Professor Laurence Katz of Harvard has recently written, "I have read over your paper with interest. You present some intriguing ideas and make the case for Concordian economics. But I must conclude that your engaging paper is not a good fit for the QJE."

Gorga has two petitions on the Internet: One is designed to "Mend the Fed"; the other to "Defuse the Bomb" of a financial crash at any stage in its development. He has been described as an economist for the modern world.

During fifty years of research and publication, 27 of them powerfully assisted by Professor Franco Modigliani, a Nobel Laureate in economics at MIT, Dr. Gorga has developed a new system of thought in which everything is logically and technically related to everything else. There are three major component elements to this system: Concordian economics, Somism, and Relationalism.

Concordian economics offers an integration of economic theory, policy, and practice; Somism integrates the Individual in Society; Relationalism presents Rationalism in full bloom, by integrating—through Relational Logic and Relational Epistemology—the foundational elements of all the sciences into a common mental framework.

From a very practical point of view, all this work accomplishes a single aim: It transforms the "dismal science" of economics into The Economics of Jubilation.

>>>

Gorga holds a Ph.D. in Political Science from the University of Naples and an M.A. in International Relations from the Johns Hopkins School of Advanced International Studies (SAIS). The University of Naples is the University of Thomas Aquinas, Giambattista Vico, Alfonso de Liguori, and Benedetto Croce. His Alma Mater was the first University in Europe to establish a separate chair for economics (separate from the moral sciences).

>>>

He was born in the Deep South of southern Italy, Roccadaspide (SA), in the year of the Lord, as they used to say, 1935, during the dictatorship of Mussolini. That was the midst of the Great Depression, which was soon followed by WW II—and the hoarding of basic foodstuff. The smell of burned flesh is still in his nostrils; and the pains of hunger too widespread to discuss. Clearly, he has deep reasons to be a practicing economist and nonviolent activist

>>>

He is married to the beautiful and extremely analytical Joan M. Gorga; they live in a colonial house at the center of the oldest fishing port in the nation—and the place of birth of the Massachusetts Bay Colony, Gloucester, MA; they have one son, Jonathan, who is a writer and owns the smallest comics bookstore on earth, in New York City, on Carmine Street. Where else?

www.ingramcontent.com/pod-product-compliance
Lightning Source LLC
Chambersburg PA
CBHW040854110726
48005CB00001B/65